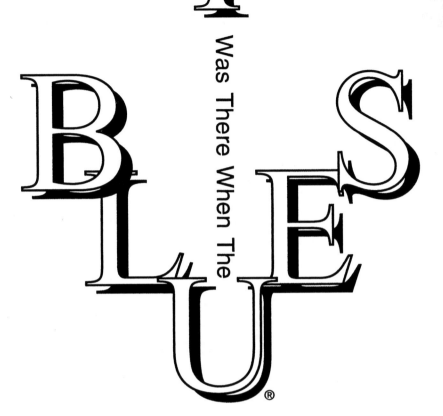

I

Was There When The

B L U E S

Was Red Hot

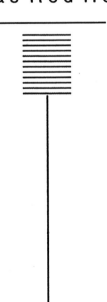

F e r n a n d o J o n e s

JONES TOMES

Cover Designer Fernando Jones

Photographer Paul Natkin

Publicist Phoebe Tree

Advisor Lana Cromwell Jones

Distributor The Ingram Book Group

This book has been used by students securing Ph.D. degrees from:
Indiana University, University of Maryland, Northwestern University & Union Institute

Order Online
Amazon.Com • Borders.Com • BluesKids.Com

Fan Mail
BluesNewz@Aol.Com

Library of Congress Catalog Card Number 90-91550
10 9 8 7 6 5 4
ISBN 0-962-5357-1-0
Borders Bookstore BINC Number 7402764

© All Rights Reserved
1988, 2004 Fernando Jones

For book signings, distribution deals, concert tours, speaking engagements, symposiums, etcetera, please contact us: The Jones Publishing Group c/o Blues Book, 10754 Rhodes, Chicago, IL 60628, 773-995-6389.

All rights reserved. No part of this publication may be reproduced or used in any form or by any means (graphic, electronic, or mechanical, including photocopying, recording, taping, or information storage and retrieval systems) without written permission of the publisher.

Dedicated to my inspiration, motivation, and full time elation
Lana, my wife.

I Was There When The Blues Was Red Hot reflects the visions and commitments of a young Black male to his roots. Fernando Jones inherited the Blues as a musical expression, philosophy, and culture. His book displays his love for Blues in its grittiness as well as its lyrical celebration of life. At a time when many young Blacks suffer from historical amnesia, Jones in I Was There When The Blues Was Red Hot links himself with the aspirations of his group in a language tough enough and wholesome enough to do justice. I am sure his words, observations, insights, reflections, and analysis will broaden the appreciation of Blues.
-Professor Sterling D. Plumpp, University of Illinois at Chicago

I think the book is great! It's inspiring to the future of the Blues. Fernando is an asset to the music as well as a pioneer. His music is traditional enough to hold the current generation and creative enough to spark the interest of the future one.
-Shirli Dixon, *Willie Dixon's Blues Heaven Foundation*

Fernando Jones epitomizes a new movement in Black youth towards rediscovery and love of our musical roots in Africa in captivity. Mr. Jones is an Afrocentric Renaissance man. I thank the gods of our ancestors for his existence.
-L.T. Beauchamp, *Literati Internationale* publisher

The book expresses the same qualities of enthusiasm and truth as he talks about his heroes, his own development as a performer as a song writer, and his efforts to promote the music he loves to Chicago and the rest of the world.
-Tom Allen, *Chippewa Valley Blues Coalition News*

Fernando you know how important it is to preserve the true spirit of the Blues for those who come after us. I'm proud of you for your initiative. Keep on keepin' on. This is an earnest first effort by a promising young brother.
-Ralph Metcalfe, *Bluesologist and Educator*

Fernando Jones' sound is very much his own personal sound, made up of phrases different from anyone else's, and for the moment he cannot be compared to anyone else.
-Angelo Morini, *Il Blues Magazine*

Fernando is an accomplished player and historian of the Blues in Chicago. Fernando also served as an advisor to the school in the development of its own Blues School.
-Michael J. Miles, *Director of the Old Town School of Folk Music*

Fernando is not allowing the Blues to be buried with the past. He is definitely playing an intricate role in the progression for the future generation. It's so American!
-Jimmy Dunlop, *Jim Dunlop Guitar Effects & Accessories*

I think you are pushin' an issue and that's good. You've got a good heart and mind. You are a unique person and I like that. And I like what you are doing.
-Junior Wells, *Godfather of the Blues*

You can feel proud that your efforts have had a positive influence on the lives of several hundred students.
-Mary T. Feldman, *Blues in the Schools Trust Fund*

This book is very informative and I hope the world gets a chance to see it. It'll be the treat of your life.
-Tina Mayfield, *The International Blues Society*

I knew you could play, but I didn't know you could play like that.
-Lefty Dizz, *Blues Legend*

Fernando Jones' other literary works include:

Over 300 songs published with Broadcast Music, Inc. (BMI)

Who's gonna shovel the snow? (Fiction)

The Blues Kids of America Activities Book

<u>Interactive Theatrical Experiences</u>
I Was There When The Blues Was Red Hot
Blue Eyed Blues
Why do U Like me? U don't even know me.
The Train Game
I Feel With My Hands
Blues For Jesus (Co-writer)

Foreword
by Dr. Frances G. Carroll
University of Illinois Board of Trustees Member

Fernando Jones is a creative, gifted, and multitalented individual whose love for the Blues has permeated his being. His energy and enthusiasm easily transmit that love to others. His unique style of translating the Blues into an educational experience has enhanced the learning of thousands of school age children across our nation.

This book commands the attention of the young and old, and places him among the outstanding music educators. Fernando Jones presents the Blues' history in a clean and wholesome genre that can be internalized by the reader. Most impressive about this dynamic historical research, on a traditional American musical style, is the many outstanding references to situations and circumstances familiar to diverse readers. The chronological review of African American History, pain and suffering unfolding in the creating of a style of music known as the Blues is authenticated in *I Was There When The Blues Was Red Hot*.

Reading this book makes me emotional and motivates me to continue to keep our story alive and reestablishes the importance of passing this history down to our children. *I Was There When The Blues Was Red Hot* highlights the magnitude of Fernando's intenseness of his love for the Blues. This love can be attributed to his genealogy, of course. This writing is evidently a personal commitment to telling, selling, and enlightening the students across the nation, especially African American students about the rich style of music made by Black folk.

I Was There When The Blues Was Red Hot frames the origin of the Blues in the belly of slavery and gives new meaning to every phrase of song. Testimonies from public figures, from educator to entertainer, document the value of the music style of the Blues and reconfirm what we already know. Every African American household should own a copy of *I Was There When The Blues Was Red Hot.*

x

Fernando Jones grew up in a house where Blues music dominated the family record player. A number of prominent Chicago Blues artists are members of his family. Foree Superstar is Fernando's eldest brother. Foree had first taken him into the world-famous Theresa's Lounge by the time he was five years old. He thus acquired a love for the Blues. His adoration of the music led him in two directions. The first being the self-instruction of several musical instruments, initially the guitar and drums, and more recently, the harmonica. The second direction led him to the undertaking of this project.

Fernando prepared himself for his current role of Blues hierophant at the University of Illinois at Chicago. He graduated in 1987. While there, he was involved in a number of African American classes, workshops and symposiums under the tutelage of professors Grace S. Holt and Sterling D. Plumpp. Also, while still a student, Fernando organized landmark festivals that showcased the talents of many of Chicago's seminal music and heritage performers. He was able to secure the patronage from the likes of Buddy Guy, Magic Slim, Foree Superstar, KoKo Taylor, Muddy Waters, Jr., and Junior Wells. As an alumnus, he continued to produce programs at the University, such as The First Annual Blues & Heritage Festival in the fall of 1989 that was sponsored by the UIC Black Alumni Association.

He has dedicated himself to recognizing the Blues Masters without exploiting them and to cataloging their lives without engaging in myth-making or slander. This project also stems from his deeply felt sense of irony that here in Chicago, the Blues capitol of the world, the same music Masters who are celebrated elsewhere seem to be ignored here.

His book, *I Was There When The Blues Was Red Hot,* is a labor of love. This project involved more than 10 years of doing research, securing trust and conducting interviews. It meant going anywhere and everywhere *the music* was being played in the Chicagoland area. This included bars, clubs, festivals, and even Downtown street corners.

In the process of compiling this data, Fernando still found the time to write and perform the music he cares so much about. *I Was There When The Blues Was Red Hot* offers a young African American Bluesman's perspective of the Chicago Blues scene. It is a thorough examination of the lives of several Bluesmen and Blueswomen and a tribute to the genius of the music they help sustain.

-Troy Norman

1619

In 1619, the first enslaved Africans were brought to Jamestown, Virginia by the Dutch.

1600s (Enslaved in America)
Field Hollers, Street Cries, Spirituals, Work Songs

1880s & 1890s
Folk and Rural Blues, Ragtime, Boogie Woogie

1900s
Jazz (New Orleans Blues)

1920
Downhome Blues, Vaudeville Blues

1930s Gospel Music
(Creator Bluesman Thomas A. Dorsey)

1940s
Urban Blues, Rhythm & Blues, BeBop

1945
Post War Blues

1950s (Up Tempo Blues)
Rock & Roll

1960s
Soul (Smooth Blues)

Late 1960s
Blues Rock (Blue Eyed Blues), Post modern

1970s
Contemporary Blues and Gospel, Disco, Funk

Late 1970s
Jazz Fusion, Rap & Hip Hop (New York City)

1980s
Techno (Detroit), House (Chicago)

1990
New Jack Swing (East Coast)

There are undoubtedly dozens of other music forms that could have been on this list, however, these are some of the more popular styles birthed from the Blues.

Intro

Born in Chicago on February 7, 1964, *the Year of the Dragon*, under the Zodiac sign of Aquarius, was I. Yes, Fernando is my real name. That year, the cost to send a letter first class was 5¢; an ounce of gold, 35¢; admission to the movies, 93¢; Lyndon B. Johnson was President, and Richard J. Daley was the Mayor of my hometown. The day before my 6th birthday, my uncle, Jackson Stack, took me to the Goldblatt's Department Store at 47th & Ashland and bought me my first electric guitar and amp. The amp was the size of a shoebox, and the guitar was a sunburst Tiesco, but you'd have thought it was a vintage Fender Telecaster the way it was treasured. I've been strummin' ever since.

During my childhood, our family went down South to Mississippi at least once a year. If there were a funeral we'd go twice. Going to Mississippi was a rite of passage. In those days, Black folks from the city would go down South by car, Greyhound bus, or Amtrak. We never heard of anybody flying. We'd take perfectly seasoned fried chicken wrapped in foil, fruit, soda, potato chips, and the Blues would be blasting on the 8-track tape player. Every now and then my folks would bring a jar or two of corn whiskey back. That's a different book. Back then, good radio stations were far and few in between on the road. For some Mississippians Chicago was their proverbial *Promised Land.*

On Saturday, June 18, 1988, Sugar Blue invited me to perform a harmonica duet with him at Wise Fools Pub on Lincoln Avenue in Chicago. A conversation from that night sparked this project. After a week of collecting data, my sister, Earnestine, loaned me her typewriter. Later, computers were made available to me by my cousin, Vicky, Troy Norman, and Emory and Paulette Smith.

This publication was written for, and is dedicated to, the preservation and cultivation of this traditional African American art form. Though it is mathematically impossible to recognize and pay tribute to everyone who has done something to advance this movement, I do realize that many folks have died penniless, lonely, and without proper recognition in spite of their paramount contributions. And for that, I thank them. *I Was There* will respectfully introduce you to musicians, historians, disk jockeys, recording artists, club owners, promoters, philosophers, fans, and even kids. Blues Kids.

As per the book title, in no way does it suggest that a moratorium has been placed on this music and culture. Nor does it suggest that I, the author, have "seen it all" or "know it all." If anything, this entitlement champions the future and celebrates the past through eyewitness accounts from many compassionate and unselfish contributors. Hopefully, this book will add greater insight into he world of the Blues.

Some Prominent Pre-War (World War II)
Vaudeville / Classic Blues Queens

Josephine Baker, Lucille Bogan, Ida Cox, Nellie Florence, Lillian Glinn, Lil Greene, Lucille Hegamin, Rosa Henderson, Bertha "Chippie" Hill, Helen Humes, Alberta Hunter, Sara Martin, Josie Miles, Lizzie Miles, Memphis Minnie, Gertrude Pridgett a.k.a. "Ma" Rainey, Bessie Smith, Clara Smith, Mamie Smith, Trixie Smith, Queen Victoria Spivey, Beulah "Sippie" Wallace, Ethel Waters, Edith Wilson, and others.

Some Prominent Post-World War II
Blues Queens to Now

Mildred Bailey, Etta Baker, LaVern Baker, Ruth Brown, Ann Cole, Elizabeth Cotten, Sugar Pie De Santo, Etta James, Ella Johnson, Jessie Mae Hemphill, Billie Holiday, Big Maybelle, Little Ester Phillips, KoKo Taylor, Carla Thomas, Willie Mae "Big Mama" Thornton, Dinah Washington, Katie Webster, Betty Wright, Mama Yancey, and others.

•

Some Prominent Pre-War (World War II)
Downhome / Country Blues Kings

Kokomo Arnold, Ed Bell, Scrapper Blackwell, Blind Blake, Willie "Big Bill" Broonzy, Gabriel Brown, Willie Brown, Leroy Carr, Dr. Clayton, John Creach, Reverend Gary Davis, Sleepy John Estes, Blind Boy Fuller, Guitar Gabriel, Blind Roosevelt Graves, William Christopher "W.C." Handy, Buddy Boy Hawkins, Sam "Lightnin'" Hopkins, Son House, Homesick James, Skip James, Blind Lemon Jefferson, George Washington Johnson, Lonnie Johnson, Robert Johnson, Tommy Johnson, Booker T. Laury, Hudie "Leadbelly" Ledbetter, Furry Lewis, Mead Lux Lewis, Mississippi Fred McDowell, Blind Willie McTell, the Memphis Jug Band, Little Brother Montgomery, "Hambone" Willie Newbern, Charley Patton, Robert Petway, Yank Rachell, William "Pa" Rainey, Speckled Red, the Mississippi Sheiks, Johnny Shines, Memphis Slim, Sunnyland Slim, Henry Sloan, Clarence "Pinetop" Smith, Roosevelt "The Honeydripper" Sykes, Johnnie Temple, Henry Thomas, Son Thomas, Peetie Wheatstraw, Robert Pete Williams, John Lee "Sonny Boy" Williamson, Jimmy Yancey and others.

Some Prominent Post-World War II
Blues Kings to Now

Albert Ammons, Chuck Berry, Bobby "Blue" Bland, Zu Zu Bollin, Lonnie Brooks, Charles Brown, Roy Brown, Clarence Carter, Leonard "Baby Doo" Caston, John Cephus, Nat "King" Cole, Johnny "Clyde" Copeland, Pee Wee Crayton, Larry Davis, Walter Davis, Jimmy Dawkins, Bo Diddley, Bill Doggett, Floyd Dixon, Willie Dixon, Fats Domino, Big Joe Duskin, Buddy Guy, Slim Harpo, Peppermint Harris, Wynnonie Harris, Al Hibbler, Z.Z. Hill, John Lee Hooker, Big Walter Horton, Ivory Joe Hunter, J.B. Hutto, Little Walter Jacobs, Elmore James, John Jackson, Louis Jordan, Albert King, B.B. King, Freddie King, J.B. Lenoir, Baby Face Leroy, Meade Lux Lewis, Joe Liggins, Robert Lockwood, Jr., Professor Longhair, Willie Mabon, Jimmy McCracklin, Brownie McGhee, Big Jay McNeely, Percy Mayfield, Amos Milburn, Alex "Rice" Miller (Sonny Boy Williamson #2), Roy Milton, Johnny Otis, Little Junior Parker, Pinetop Perkins, Lonnie Pitchford, Snooky Pryor, Jimmy Reed, Otis Rush, Jimmy Rushing, Magic Sam, "Peg Leg" Sam, Guitar Slim, Otis Spann, "Pops" Staples, "Hound Dog" Taylor, Sonny Terry, Rufus Thomas, Allen Toussain't, Henry Townsend, Big Joe Turner, Aaron Thibeaux a.k.a. T-Bone Walker, Muddy Waters, Johnny "Guitar" Watson, Junior Wells, Booker (sometimes spelled Bukka) White, Josh White, Phil Wiggins, Chuck Willis, Jimmy Witherspoon, Howlin' Wolf, and others.

Acknowledgements

The Jones Family featuring Essie and Willie, Lana for being my rock, mentor, and everything, the Cromwell and Jarvis Family, global friends, cast members from all of my plays, sponsors, co-workers, the folks who bought this book originally in 1990, band mates, supporters, National Alliance of Black School Educators, Blues Kids of America, Blues in the Schools, Chicago Area Alliance of Black School Educators, Real Men Cook, Chicago Public School sites that have supported the Blues Kids program, and the American Federation of Musicians.

Dan Smith at Fender, Chip Ratliff, Harp Monster, Roy Boyd, Theresa "T" Barker, Earnestine for the name "Fernando," Jackson for the first guitar, Jack Vartoogian, Paul Natkin, the Mississippi Valley Blues Society, Dr. Grace Dawson, Dr. Frances Carroll, Dr. Fannie Gibson, Dr. Barbara Sizemore, Ms. Judith Adams & the Nancy B. Jefferson School faculty, staff, and students, Ron "O.J." Parson for the acting break, Sam Mendenhall, and Todd Stephens.

Jennifer Guy & Family for the encouragement and support, Tyrone Blackshear, David "DP" Carlson for the film version of this book, Fruteland Jackson for the web site, Charles "Gator" Hudson for the brotherhood, Butch at Bacon's hat shop on 47th Street for the *lids*, Chuck D. of Public Enemy for appreciating the Blues publicly and acknowledging its global cultural, musical impact, James Trotter at One-Stop Auto, First Class II Productions, Phoebe Tree for the PR, and Ben Edelberg for the film.

Sugar Blue, Sterling Plumpp, Willie Dixon, Otis Williams, Dr. Caleb Dube, Troy Norman, Foree Superstar, Nova Parham, Pevin Everett, Dr. Abena Joan, Brown, Runako Jahi, Alan Swyer, Tom Marker, Steve Cushing, Barry Dolins, Grace Holt, Steve Cobb, Eddie Butler, Michael Grossman, John Primer, Ralph Metcalfe, Big Bill Collins, Rahsaan Morris, Dr. Susan Oehler, Darrell "Creasebone" Creasy, Felton Crews, Carl Wright, Carl "$2" Vanoy for our theatrical production & the Vanoy-Jordan Family, Des Doran & Family, ETA, Dr. Hoffman and the North Kenwood Oakland Charter School, Marie Dixon & the Blues Heaven family, Denise and Jill at the Blues Exchange, Gallery 37, Patrick Doody for the studio time, Leilane Linn at Kinko's for the PDF files, Amazon.Com, Beverly Mitchell and Mary at Lightning Source, Mark Monahan of Ottawa's Blues in the Schools, the Simply Wow crew, Kelvin "Rappn" Tate, and Ms. Cronin at Borders Bookstore.

•Collecting data for this book included extensive research and countless hours of making sure that I was not telling the same story told hundreds of times before. In addition to the aforementioned, my research also consisted of interviews and visits to the bookstores and libraries—just to see what was out there. The findings were slim and shocking. Most of the books that I found on "Black" music/musicians (Blues, Jazz, R&B, Doo Wop, Hip-hop, etcetera) were not written by Black folks. At that point, this project became more than just a book, it became a necessity.

O N E
What is the Blues? Why does it exist?

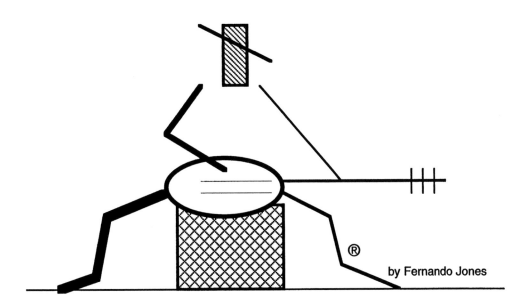

by Fernando Jones

Rooted in the African tradition of call-and-response, the Blues, mother and father of Jazz, Rock & Roll, Rhythm & Blues, Gospel, and even Hip-hop music, is an indigenous African American art form. It's also a cultural institution filled with volumes of autobiographical, economical, sociological, and historical information expressed through the arts in disciplines such as, but not limited to music, literature, dance, and the theatre.

Musically, for more than seventy-five years, the Blues has been an ambassadorial tool of goodwill from America to the world. Culturally, it's been embraced and consumed globally just like McDonald's hamburgers and Coca~Cola. Some scholars have considered the Blues to be an artistic phenomenon due to its uncanny ability to transcend and address controversial issues such as race, class, gender, politics, and even socio-economics.

Woven into the fabric of this country, this art form is nothing short of an in-depth autobiography documenting America. Though created on southern plantations by enslaved Africans and their descendents through moans, groans, street cries, ring shouts, and field hollers induced by circumstances and conditions, each generation continually redefines this music and culture. Blues songs generally tell complete stories in three verses exposing one's truths, tragedies, triumphs, trials and tribulations. Here is a chart with basic song themes. Use this chart to make up songs of your own.

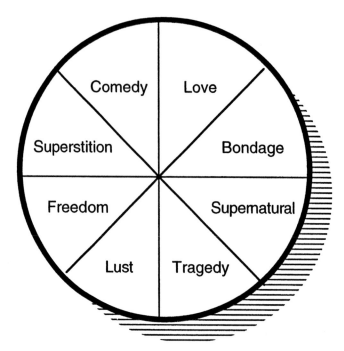

One of the fundamentals of Blues music is the call-and-response. Though an Africanism, call-and-response is in everything from nursery rhymes to Country & Western music. Harvard University Professor Henry Louis Gates, Jr. said this in a December 12, 1996 *New York Times* article written by Dinitia Smith: "Embedded in all aspects of this oral tradition is the pattern of call-and-response. It is the structural principle of worship, the unbroken center of secular and sacred forms. It's never not been there." Below is a sample of the call-and-response using the AAB structure. Example: *The Blues Spares None* by Fernando Jones.

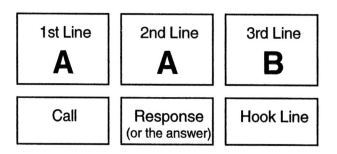

(A)   The Call (person 1)
       I tumble like a tumbleweed, and roll like a rollin' stone.

(A)   Response (repeat by the group)
       Hey, I tumble like a tumbleweed, and roll like a rollin' stone.

(B)   Hook Line (everybody together)
       You'll never see, see me crumble.
       And you'll never know the Blues I've known.

In the film inspired by this book Willie Dixon said, "The Blues are the true facts of life that are expressed in words and song, feeling and inspiration, and most people don't know this. People have always tried to make [the] Blues a negative something, but the Blues are the true facts of life. I feel like if anybody has ever had the experience of what Blues are, and what Blues is supposed to be, has been me. Not just because it's the Blues, but because of the experience and knowing what the Blues means and being taught about the Blues all my life. You see, most people have always had the wrong conception of the Blues." In the '20s, the Blues was also called "Race music." The late Professor Otis Williams from University of Maryland said the Blues is "the cutting edge of our culture."

Sociological experiences that influence how Blues music is made.

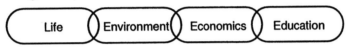

Life | Environment | Economics | Education

Slavery: Seeds of the Blues

To better understand this music and culture, let's talk about the institutionalized manipulation of the enslaved Africans in America because this situation created the Blues idiom. Slavery enslaved the body, mind, and spirit in some cases, too. The Blues is a testament of a people's courage and strength to overcome extinction. Classism, ignorance, and White supremacy helped inspire, shape, and advance this musical and cultural movement, too. It's ironic that something so inhumane could produce an art form so beautiful. In 1889, the term "Blues" was first used to describe the alleged "blue" style of folk music performed by rural Black itinerant musicians.

The United Slaves of America by Fernando Jones
Ivory, gold, and tribal bodies stolen from Africa's great body of work
Remains of stained etchings in the minds of sagacious elders.
Bitter to taste in mouths of her babies,
Unbelievable, their ears as they listen.
Carrying my ancestors 'round in my suitcase
400 years of Black folk and their fears
Slaves with permanent shackles . . .
Separated by skin color;
Classism, ed-ju-ma-cation, hair texture, and zip codes.
From all the cotton jeans I wear
Granddaddy's blood innate in the stitchings
Depicting patterns of the deep South's in incomprehensibility.
For all the cotton shirts that I wear on my unbeaten back
Lies Grandma's recollection of the old days.
For all the cotton in the jeans and shirts I wear
Are only microcosms of the sacks and rows upon rows

Of cotton they picked, religiously
Once 10 tons of steel echoed in a welder's protective facemask
Now, mills are replaced by my broken back's memory of
Yesterday's 9 to 5.
From the auctioneers,
"This fine young buck has good teeth."
To "Swing low sweet chariot"
To Dr. King's "I have a dream."
Or Jesse Jackson's "I am somebody!"
    From WHITES ONLY water fountains on 100-degree days
    In Mississippi to fire hoses offensively tackling
    COLOREDS ONLY live on TV in Alabama.
    The blacker the berry, the sweeter the juice,
    Except for when it comes to me.
    Black is sometimes beautiful as good is sometimes news,
    I've got 'em and you've got 'em,
    We've all got the Blues.

Before we dive deep into the flow of this section, it's my belief that the seeds for the Blues were sewn when the first shackled Africans set their shoeless, swollen, callused, bleeding feet on the muddy and hostile shores of America, *the New World*. However, the institution of slavery dates back to Ancient Times as far as 3,500 BC. It was practiced among the powerful, privileged, and prosperous in countries such as Assyria, Babylon, China, Egypt/Kemet, India, and Persia.

The master/slave concept is based on a person's, or institution's philosophy that promotes supremacy and dominance over another using a combination of psychology, force, and intimidation with the intention of gaining something for nothing. In other words, one must have "someone" or "something" beneath him or her in order to make them feel important.

A classic example of the disregard for African life is illustrated on a plaque in the DuSable Museum of African American History, Chicago. In brief, document states that sharks had been known to trail some of the merchant ships in anticipation of the inevitable . . . African bodies dropped overboard into the Atlantic Ocean during the Middle Passage.

In addition to bodies (also known as Black gold), items such as diamonds, ivory, gold, art, exotic animals, artifacts, timber, cottonseed, rubber, coal, palm oil, coffee, wheat, corn, rice, sugarcane, nuts, fruit, tobacco, copper, lead, uranium, and zinc were also taken. Technological information pertaining to agriculture was also taken during Africa's rape.

In 1619, the Dutch brought the first enslaved Africans to Jamestown, Virginia. The enslaved were known as the *twenty Negars*. I guess this is what B.B. King is talking about when he sings:

> *Everybody wants to know*
> *Why I sing the Blues.*
> *Yes, I say, 'Everybody wants to know*
> *Why I sing the Blues.'*
> *Well, I've been around a long time . . .*
> *Really have paid my dues.*
> *When I first got the Blues*
> *They brought me over on a ship.*
> *Men were standing over me,*
> *And a lot, Lawd, with a whip.*
> *Everybody wants to know*
> *Why I sing the Blues.*
> *Well, I've been around a long time.*
> *I really have paid my dues.*

African slaves were even given to the Pope as benevolence acts in exchange for his blessing(s). African kings supported and fueled the trade, too, by selling some of their own personal slaves and prisoners of war to traders and merchants. The enslaved Africans were traded for goods such as fabric, molasses, weaponry, and alcohol. This cruel act of inhumanity stripped many folks of their families, heritage, cultural and spiritual beliefs, property, native language(s)/dialects, and freedom.

By the 1650s, the British, and French were participating in the slave trade. This marked the beginning of the colonization process of what we now call Africa of which was named after the Roman conqueror General Africanus. Africa's former name was Alkebulan. That means *land of Black people*.

Africans, primarily specialists in agriculture from Senegal and Gambia, were brought here in dark, damp, malodorous ship bottoms indigent servants to work the land. Once here, the enslaved worked on plantations in areas such as Alabama, Arkansas, New Jersey, North Carolina, South Carolina, Delaware, Florida, Georgia, Kentucky, Louisiana, Maryland, Mississippi, Missouri, Texas, and Virginia. Africans were also taken to (and sold in) Cuba, Jamaica, Mexico, and Saint Domingue now called Haiti).

Malcolm X had this to say about the misuse of Blacks in America: "If you are the son of a man who had a wealthy estate, and you inherited your father's estate, you have to pay the debts that your father incurred. The only reason the present generation of White Americans are in the position of economic strength is [that] their fathers worked our fathers/mothers for over 400 years with no pay." From inception, the enslaved found themselves on foreign and hostile grounds taking orders from people who didn't have their best interest at heart. They were brought to America against their will and labeled property.

Keep in mind that the enslaved were not all necessarily from the same tribes, or spoke the same language(s). And to add insult to injury, the drum (usually made from large hollowed out cedar tree trunks covered with animal skin, and secured with rope), of which had the ability to transcend their many different languages and dialects had been taken away, therefore, a new form of communication was created. Injustices like this helped birth the Blues through field hollers, litanies, and chants. These actions made conditions on the plantations seem more bearable. Professor Sterling D. Plumpp, a former instructor of mine at the University of Illinois at Chicago, said, "Blues music was originally sung to an audience that shared the same experiences of the singer. It was never always sad, and it was never always funny, but it did talk very honestly about experiences that the singer had experienced. Just as the preacher who was able to manipulate the symbolism of the secular likes of people in the church, the Blues was able to manipulate the symbolism of the secular likes of the people in the Blues clubs."

The United Slaves of America (Part II)
The tongues of ten million African slaves lost at sea
Moaning blue notes of call-and-response
From one mouth,
Trapped in the belly of the Atlantic Ocean
Wallowing in its unrest a memory refusing to be digested
And released through the ocean's bowels
A memory of truth
From Africa's knee to the 40 acres & a mule y'all forgot
From the county farms housed with striped, clueless victims
To historically Black Colleges
We stand tall, the United Slaves of America!

It is important to know that some of our enslaved Africans in America that "ran away" from the plantations were given shelter by our Native American brothers and sisters. There they found refuge in music, culture, and community.

The late Grace Holt founder of the Black Studies program at the University of Illinois at Chicago, said, "We had a lack of self-image for the most part, we were illiterate, penniless, powerless, and landless. From this came the psychological damage and cultural deprivation. Over the course of time we were programmed to believe we were dispensable. The same method that the White slave owners used to suppress the slaves, the slaves reversed the roles to free their minds. The *church* was the highest symbol of our moral authority. The church figures like the preachers and ministers were our hierarchy, so we looked to them for the answers to the abolishment of slavery."

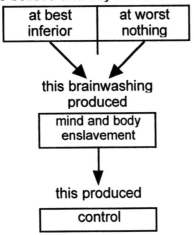

Early on in African American History, we were taught to believe and buy the lie that we were:

| at best inferior | at worst nothing |

this brainwashing produced

| mind and body enslavement |

this produced

| control |

Under an American sky those enslaved worked rhythmically and systematically from sunup to sundown without question or refutation For example, some pregnant women even gave birth while working the fields. It wasn't uncommon to see a woman out there with a baby in her stomach, one in her arm sucking and tugging on her breast, and another at her side. Some mothers even suffocated their newborns in efforts to spare them the wretched hand of slavery.

Oh, my Lawd	*Oh, my Lawd.*
Please save my soul.	*Please save my soul.*
Work done got hard.	*Work done got hard.*
And I done got old.	*Done got old.*

Dr. Ronald Myers said, "Now remember that the music that the African American's experienced in America came out in a form, whether we call it Blues, Gospel, or Jazz, that expressed a basic human soul expression. The first inflection of this experience came, in terms of White folks, on the plantations. It began to have a sociological impact in the segregated South as the slave gained freedom and began to move off the plantation. Remember, there were a lot of

White people who were poor and also were having a hard time, and if you understand the roots of Country music in terms of the slave, really, Country music and Cajun music goes back again to the experience of the slave."

International development specialist Des Doran said, "The Blues is about suffering by the Black in America, either as communities or as individuals. It is worth nothing that the suffering was not always imposed by the White majority; often it was brought on by the mistakes of one's own making."

•Here's a sample of what a field holler sounds like written by the author.
Mr. Charlie, Mr. Charlie don't you break my back.
 Mr. Charlie, Mr. Charlie don't you break my back.
'Cause my head is strong and my skin is Black.
 'Cause my head is strong and my skin is Black.
If I never see a piece of cotton again.
 If I never see a piece of cotton again.
I'll shake hands with the cotton gin.
 I'll shake hands with the cotton gin.

While enslaved, Black folks generally worked either the fields or in the slave owner's house as domestics in roles such as servants, nannies, cooks, and, yes, even concubines.

Can you imagine it being against the law for a man to provide for and protect his family? Well, during slavery the African American male was stripped of that birthright. His inability to exercise such inalienable rights as father, leader, and provider, during those terrible times, must have left his woman feeling defenseless and quite vulnerable. At times he must have felt worthless. However, preacher Nat Turner, born on a Virginia plantation, was encouraged to become educated and fight slavery by his grandmother.

Turner felt that he had a calling from God to free Black folks. In 1831, He and some of his missionaries led a bloody revolt in Jerusalem, Virginia murdering fifty-seven Whites in freedom's name.

Keep in perspective that on January 1, 1863, a little over thirty years later, President Abraham Lincoln issued the Emancipation Proclamation. By the Civil War's end in 1865, four million enslaved Americans of African descent were allegedly freed, therefore, turning many of us into tenant farmers and sharecroppers. What were our other options?

Here is a breakdown (from the 1860s) of how many enslaved Africans were in America and the states: Alabama (435,000), Arkansas (111,000),

Delaware (2,000), Florida (62,000), Georgia (482,000), Kentucky (225,000), Louisiana (332,000), Maryland (87,000), Mississippi (437,000), Missouri (115,000), New Jersey (1,000), North Carolina (331,000), South Carolina (402,000), Tennessee (276,000), Texas (183,000), and Virginia (481,000). Those enslaved made-up nearly one-third of the United States' population.

By the end of World War II (1945), thousands of Blacks, uneducated and unskilled as industrial laborers, migrated from the South in search of the *Promised Land,* the *free* North. Due to the increase of lynchings in the South and the presumption of better job opportunities in the industrial plants and factories up North, the choice for those who left was easy. Once here, some found it to be Heavenly, while others found the "big city" harsh, cold, unfriendly, and tantamount to slavery. Here are a few of the more popular places Blacks migrated North to: Baltimore, Chicago, Cleveland, Detroit, Indianapolis, Kansas City, Memphis, Nicodemus, Philadelphia, Richmond, St Louis, Washington, DC, and New York (Harlem and Brooklyn). Some journeyed West as far as Los Angeles.

When Black folks migrated from the South (primarily Mississippi, my parents' home state, Alabama, Georgia, Arkansas, and Louisiana) to Chicago many of them were armed with only their hopes and dreams of a better tomorrow for their families. They settled either on the town's West or South side. The West side was simply knows as the "the West side" and the South side was called Bronzeville, Black Metropolis—a city within a city. Bronzeville had a Black operated hospital, banks, insurance companies, churches, professional athletic and civic organizations, newspapers, cosmetic companies, funeral homes, schools, real estate companies, grocery stores, diners, dance halls, ballrooms, night clubs, and even an organized gambling lottery game called *policy.*

What does the Devil have to do with the Blues?

In the 1930s, many preachers and church folks classified the Blues as *Devil's Music.* Some still subscribe to that indoctrination. Founder of the International Blues Society Tina Mayfield (widow of the Poet Laureate of the Blues Percy Mayfield) said, "The Devil ain't never made no music. He was in the choir, in Heaven, and he messed that up." In an interview by Dr. Leon Finney on the *Another Perspective* TV show Pops Staples of the Staples Singers said, "Some people who play the Blues are better Christians than those that go to church."

"Professor" Eddie Lusk and his dad, a Pentecostal minister, didn't speak to each other for over five years because he played the Blues. "I came up from Arkansas to Chicago," Eddie said, "and happened to land on the street called 43rd Street which was very famous for the Blues. That street held a club called Pepper's Lounge and you would see all of your South side Bluesmen like Buddy Guy, Junior Wells, Washboard Sam, or Hound Dog Taylor. All those kinds of *cats* would hang out, man, [and] they would play this club called Pepper's Lounge which was at 43rd & Vincennes, and by me being a church boy I would sneak down there at night while my parents would be sleep and I'd listen to this music. It was like, wow, man, I never heard no music like this because I was a church musician playin' *Near My God Oh Thee, Oh Happy Day,* and such.

"I used to mimic playin' the Blues at church and my father would say, 'Boy that's Blues music. That ain't nothin' but some *Devil music.*' I was enhanced about the music because it was all about telling a story and was all about history. So I'd try and play Blues while the choir would be singin', and my mother, she was into the music there and she was the person who taught me my first key which was B flat, and I'd play everything in B flat. So If the choir was singin' in C, I was playin' in B flat. I was playin' Blues runs in church while the Gospel was goin' on, and what happened was the people enjoyed it because most of them listened to Blues music, too." Eddie can be seen in the film adaptation of this book.

The Reverend Dr. Ronald Myers had a similar background. He wrote his publication <u>Jazz Improvisation in Amos</u>: "This was a common belief and expression that was prevalent in the church when I was a child. I can remember vividly being scolded by my mother for banging on the piano as I innocently tried to stimulate the intricate polyrhythmic expressions I heard on late night Jazz radio and at home. My mother was the church musician and my father was a former Jazz nightclub singer."

We know Jazz and Rock & Roll came from Blues, and as unfathomable as it may seem, Gospel music did, too. Thomas A. Dorsey (a.k.a. Georgia Tom, piano player for Tampa Red, Ma Rainey, and Bessie Smith) changed the sound, shape, and structure of church music when he created Gospel music.

In showing the link between Gospel and the Blues, Alan Swyer, producer of *the Ray Charles Story,* expressed himself outside Harvelle's night club in

Santa Monica, California by crediting Ray Charles as the music "preacher" who married Rhythm & Blues to Gospel music with the song *Hallelujah, I Love Her So.* Alan said, "When that hit record came out several prominent Black clergymen demanded that the song be banned from the airways, and the stores immediately made it a *must hear* for teenagers. So it became the first great cross-over record; Ray being *Ray,* never wanting to duck controversy, went a step further, thereafter, by adding a vocal group named the Cookies and renamed them the Raelets and brought in [the] call-and-response which is clearly something used in church music. In Gospel music listen to James Cleveland and you'll hear it. Without getting any credit for it, he changed the world because the South arguably would have stayed rooted in a kind of pre-Civil War mentality had it not been for Ray Charles.

"Why is it important musically? R&B had pretty much hit the wall. People were doing the same thing again and again and again. When that happens either something dies, or somebody does somethin' really new. He found something new by bringing in something old directly from the church that he'd adored in his childhood. Ray said, 'I don't wanna just do music as product. I wanna do music that has heart and soul.' Frankly, without Ray who knows if there'd be any Soul music?

"He chose not just to be an entertainer, but to be an adventurer. He feels, to this day, that anything he sings is an expression of him. And if it's an expression of what he feels in his heart how can it be bad? And if he loves the church, how can it be sacrilegious to bring in the church's music? A close friend of his was Archie Brownlee, leader of the Five Blind Boys, arguably the greatest Gospel singer of all time, and people say that's heresy. How can that be heresy? Here is a man who loved Gospel music, and put his money where his mouth is, so to speak, by marrying a Gospel singer and by hanging out with his dear friend, Archie Brownlee, who loved what Ray did. It's clear that Aretha Franklin brought the church into everything she sang as well, and she credits Ray Charles for opening the door for that."

By the 1950s, just thirty years after the birth of the recording industry, the sound, shape, texture and face of this music had changed tremendously. The music that once told stories of trains, cotton fields, oppression, and poverty now boasted of automobiles, the big city, freedom, and pockets full of money. The rural Blues infused with urban experiences is what produced Rock & Roll. Rock music captured the spirit, angst, recklessness, and rebelliousness of the urban youth. At that moment, the Blues was looked at as *old folk's music.*

The term Rock & Roll was originally used in urban and rural African American communities decades before it was called a form of music. It could have meant any and everything from *getting down* with your loved one sexually to *taking care of business* to having a *natural ball.* The term Rock & Roll was lifted from the African American lexicon and applied to this new and exciting form of music.

Jesus came to town with 12 apostles and a mule.

He came to tell everybody

That the Devil's got slippery shoes.

Communication: The importance of the drum

Dr. Ronald Myers founder of the Fellowship of Creative Christian Jazz Musicians said, "When the White man would show up on a part of the land Africans would know two hundred or three hundred miles away that the White man was there. Africans would talk to each other over the drum. Africans had a sophisticated way of communicating through the drum. When the African was kidnapped and brought to America the drums were taken away. In Africa, music was a three hundred-and-sixty degree circle. Africans did everything to music. They had drum cadences for marriages, work, and every social affair. They would also communicate to each other over the talking drum. There were successful slave revolts because the African was able to communicate through the drum and get the Africans together. In America, the slave master learned quite quickly that it wasn't a good idea to let the Africans have their drums. So the drum became an intricate part of the African's expression through his hands, feet, and voice. So what happened is that in the course of the African's experience in America came a musical expression that was unique to the African experience in America."

"The drum," Dr. Abena Joan Brown said, "comes form the heart beat; that means it comes from the very essence of life. It comes from the essence of a people's soul." Master drummer Steve Cobb said, "The drums speak to our spirit in a way nothing else can."

SC: I was about four years old when I first became interested in drums. I was living on 59th & Princeston, just a couple blocks away from Englewood High School, and on this [particular] day Englewood High School's marching band marched right down the street in front of my house. They had trumpets, and tubas, and all kinds of instruments, but I was most impressed with the drummers in the drum line, because I could hear the drums coming for several blocks and I couldn't wait until they got close enough for me to see them. From that point on I've been interested in the drums.

FJ: When did you find out the drum was 'deeper' than just an instrument?

SC: I've always had an innate sense of this. In the early '70s, I played with a guitarist named Phil Upchurch and a keyboardist named Tennyson Stevens. We played at clubs on the North side [of Chicago].

Many times I had experiences which were very much like a trance. It was kind of like being on auto pilot. I was indeed playing beyond myself, and what I found was that I could feel the music take me and I played far beyond what I thought my capabilities were. I later saw how drums were used in rituals. I have seen people go into trances as a result of the music. The drums speak to our spirit in a way nothing else can.

FJ: Why is the drum so important?

SC: The drum is important because it is the vehicle through which we express aspects of our being, our rhythm. Rhythm is a crucial part of our existence, because everything in nature vibrates at different frequencies which accounts for color, density, sound, and light. In fact, the ebb and flow of the moon, stars, sun [and] everything has a rhythm and it is the drum which gives us a tool with which we can express our rhythm and attune our rhythms to the cycles of nature. So, drums are very important.

FJ: Can you explain the 'talking drums' of Africa?

SC: There are two talking drum types that I am familiar with: One is called the Atumpan and it's the talking drum from Ghana. If you have seen the movie 'Sankofa,' in the very beginning there's a drummer who was the guardian of the castle at Cape Coast. Every morning he would play the drums at sunrise. Then there's the Dondons, which is the hourglass shaped drum, and it's played by the people of Nigeria. Generally, when drummers got together and played they called it a drum talk, and it was based on a conversation. Drums have always been used to communicate.

When a particular ethnic group speaks a particular language their drum patterns and rhythms are based off of the language. So there are phrases that are commonly understood by everybody which can be translated through drums, and when those drums are played everybody knows what's being said.

FJ: If people in Africa spoke many different languages, how could a drum speak to all?

SC: If you play certain rhythms it speaks to your body and moves your spirit. You can find it. It's just like the Blues. I've played in some countries where there were language barriers, but wherever you play the Blues people respond to it almost in a similar type of way, and it's the same thing with the drums because when the drums play they tell you to do something. They tell you to move and to dance to the rhythm.

So in a real sense the drums can communicate a message regardless of what language you speak. The drum and dance are inexplicably connected to each other. When drums are played, the rhythms tell you to move. Even if you don't know how to dance you will find a connection with the rhythm. So dance and drumming are one piece no matter what culture you're from.

When drummer Nate Applewhite was asked how he felt about youngsters getting involved with this music he said, "A young drummer playing the Blues is great! I started when I was fourteen years old playing with *cats* who were older than me. That's what got me interested in playing Blues." My original drummer, André Cotton, said, "I feel the future of the Blues is in the hands of the younger generation. The road was paved for us. It's really headed in a positive direction, and it's still growing. I'm going to add my contributions and roots to the future of the Blues so that I can be a role model for the younger generation." Roy Boyd, my current drummer said, "Being a Black person . . . the Blues means everything to me."

Throughout African villages the drum is used to communicate and celebrate everything from births to burials and weddings to war. The drum can be so much more effective than a voice because it can transcend language barriers, and can travel greater distances.

$$A + B = C$$

$$\underline{\text{Life} + \text{Unfairness} =}$$

The Blues

In Chapter One, hopefully, we've shown what the Blues is from different perspectives and how it came to be. For some, prior to reading this chapter, it might have been just a form of music played by a specific group of people with specific interests and intentions. We'll talk about who plays this music and why in the next chapters. We're excited to know your thoughts. At the end of each chapter feel free to email us your comments at:

BLUESNEWZ@AOL.COM

Remember, leave no Bluesman or woman behind.

T W O
B l u e E y e d B l u e s:
Borrowed or stolen? Appreciation or appropriation?

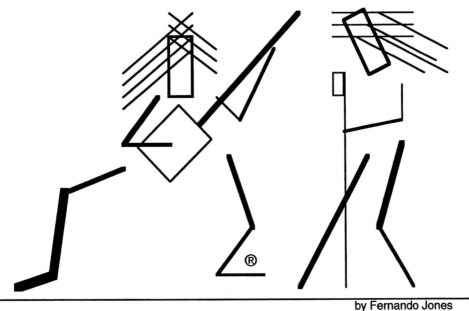

by Fernando Jones

In this section we will make distinctions between Black and White Blues musicians. Once, when the word Blues was used it was synonymous with Black folks performing it. In this section we will discuss the pros and cons of this issue with scholars, fans, musicians, disc jockeys, and the likes thereof. Though Whites have been playing the Blues commercially since the '60s some people (Blacks and Whites alike) are still unwilling to accept these interpretations as being true to form.

> *"The wholesale appreciation of Chicago's electric Blues by White rock stars in itself constitutes a tribute to the importance of its musical style. Elvis Presley, the Rolling Stones, Eric Clapton and Led Zeppelin are only more famous examples of White musicians who built careers pilfering every lick they could from Chicago Blues musicians."*
> Hands On Chicago. 1987:

As a child, I'd hear people say, "White folks stole Black folks' music" on a regular basis. As a result, I've heard Whites in the recording industry called everything from *pretenders to the throne* to *master imitators* to *culture vultures.*

Once while watching a black and white TV clip of Elvis Presley on *the Ed Sullivan Show* in a room full of Black folks someone said, "He stole that [song, vocal phrasing, and dance style] from Black folks. And the Black folks that he got it from, more than likely, can't even get a job doing their own music."

15

"Blue" Eyes, Black Roots:
A sample of 10 popular Caucasian acts
clearly rooted in African American music.

Artist(s)	Obvious Influence(s)	Music Influence(s)
The Beatles	Chuck Berry Ray Charles Little Richard	The Blues, Gospel, "Black" Rock & Roll, Rhythm & Blues and Soul ↓
The Rolling Stones	Chuck Berry Bo Diddley Willie Dixon Little Richard Ike & Tina Turner Muddy Waters Howlin' Wolf	
Billy Joel	Ray Charles	
Bonnie Raitt	Buddy Guy John Lee Hooker Aretha Franklin Sippie Wallace Junior Wells	
Rod Stewart	Same Cooke Otis Redding	
Eric Clapton	Buddy Guy Elmore James Robert Johnson Albert King B.B. King Freddie King Muddy Waters	The Blues ↓
Stevie Ray Vaughan	Bobby Bland Albert Collins Buddy Guy Jimi Hendrix Albert King B.B. King Freddie King	
ZZ Top	John Lee Hooker Muddy Waters	
Janis Joplin	Aretha Franklin	Blues and Soul
Kenny G.	Louis Armstrong John Coltrane Ronnie Laws Grover Washington	Jazz and Rhythm & Blues

Tom Marker of WXRT's Blues Breaker program said, "Even back in the early '60s those guys in Britain were big fans of the Chicago sound when they were getting their Blues thing together, themselves. Sometimes they would copy a song *lick for lick*. Mick Jagger was famous for that. He didn't just cover a song he'd copy it. He'd sing it like it was sang on the original version. At that time, the audience was predominately British and I don't think that they thought that anybody would even know that anybody had ever heard the music that they were doing. Just about every Rock band that features a hot lead guitarist is playing Blues licks, and it's hard to find a band with any kind of emphasis on the guitar where the guitarist isn't doing any Blues. Even Reggae music has Blues licks. Donald Kinsey from the Kinsey Report was lead guitarist for Bob Marley and Peter Tosh for a while."

When asked about the global attraction to this culture music researcher Michael Grossmann (an American residing in Brazil) said, "It's simple. People love good music. Other countries have their 'roots' music, and they can understand it as the ultimate form of American cultural expression. Somethin' about the Blues just grabs you."

"When the music trend changed and shifted [in the 1960s]," Jimmy Tillman said, "the Bluesman became a folk item. What happened at this particular junction was that White college students had heard some of this music and found out that some of their Rock artists, who they'd looked up to and loved, had higher regard and esteem for these Bluesmen who had been performing this music. Economically, once again, the European was making large sums of money off of these Black artists. This was back in the '60s, '62, '63 [and) all through the *Love Generation*. It was a crossover then. Blacks were not listening to it [Blues] then. The only people listening to it at that time were the White college hippie generation. You had the Filmore East and Filmore West; you'd go in there and there'd be thousands of people in these big auditoriums and here comes Muddy Waters, and he'd be the opening act for some Rock group."

When asked what is it about the Blues that makes people from other cultures and ethnic groups like it so much Dr. Frank Adams from the Alabama Jazz Hall of Fame in Birmingham, Alabama said, "To answer that question straight on, it's the richness of the music. It's the originality of the music. There's somethin' in beauty that cannot be described. It's like looking at a beautiful painting and you might not know who the creator of that painting was, but you know it's a thing of beauty. And there'll always be those who want to imitate those things or their shear beauty.

"It has been a system of codifying, but I don't think anyone can really get to the soul of the Blues unless they spend many, many years of study. And of course, the problem is for the musician, or the performer, or the very astute listener to determine the sincerity of what is offered. To a true lover of the Blues it's obvious when it's something that's stolen and is a fake. There is an ongoing effort to systematize and codify that which is not codifyable. It can't be done. But the problem is separating the fake from the real. And like a diamond versus a zircon, it's sometimes difficult for the uninitiated to make a distinction."

When asked if this music has been borrowed or stolen by our blue eyed brothers and sisters Blueswoman Barbara LeShoure emphatically said, "It is stolen! It's still stolen because they knew where the music came from. They knew it was Black cultural music. They sang about some things that they had no business knowing about being White. They [the record companies] didn't push the artists out there who created the music. I'm talking about to the degree that they could have been a 'Rolling Stones' and made the kind of money that Mick Jagger made off of it. Yes, when it's not doin' that [then] it's stolen."

And when asked about the respect issue Barbara replied, "Respect? When you say respect that means that you are going to have financial gain, as well. That's the heading of respect. There has not been any respect. All they have to do is let you know that they have kept their foot on your neck. So what good did it do? The reason the Blues is at the level it is today is because Black folks were tricked into giving their music away. If they [Whites] could really execute the music they would have done it a long time ago. You got a few White boys that are technically playing the Blues, and they're getting over."

When I asked Professor Susan Oehler from the University of Indiana at Bloomington if she thought Black Blues musicians felt eclipsed by Whites she had this to say: "This is an interesting question. Let me first preface anything that follows with the point that it's hard for me to say what anybody feels besides myself. On the basis of my field research interviewing, conversing with, and observing professional (and/or semi-professional) Blues musicians in Bloomington, Indiana (who are all men identifying their ethnicity as White

Midwesterners or European American Midwesterners) and professional Blues musicians active in Chicago's North side and South side scenes who are men and women of varied ethnicities but predominantly African American men—I can say that in Chicago, African American Blues artists often indicated that they see an inequitable system where White racial identity reflects privileged economic and positions of commercial leadership continues to affect the marketing of Black performers' music.

"While many African American Blues musicians I talked to (and keep in mind I'm a German American woman who grew up in some suburbs created out of 'White-flight') noted that anyone who learns the Blues and plays out of their true experiences has the ability to play Blues, that the idea that only African Americans have the ability to play Blues is not true. Many would bring up paradoxes that demonstrate the continued devaluation of African American Blues artists in settings where younger, White performers—covering Blues standards and original Blues that didn't stand out may even be less riveting than what's going on in networks of African American Blues performers make more rapid, more supported (in terms of the music industry), more financially lucrative headway in markets predominated by Whites. I think a related phenomenon that is interesting is that the styles of Blues that are statistically most popular among predominantly African American audiences today, known as 'Soul Blues' in marketing terms (artists like Denise LaSalle, Bobby Bland, Tyrone Davis, Z. Z. Hill) aren't being crossed over to audiences beyond African American settings. I started thinking about this when thinking about the subtle differences in repertoire in some Blues groups who play both South and North side gigs.

"If Funk and Soul oldies are now of interest to the generation that grew up with Rap crossover, which would tend to be in higher numbers on the North side, why wouldn't the Soul/R&B Blues sound sell up on the North side? I think a lot of this has do with what the predominantly White Blues audience has been taught. So this could be conceived of as a financial overshadowing, to use your term. My research shows that professional musicians in Blues pull on resources as creators of music, as people familiar with the Blues traditions, as people interacting with African American culture (even people with the least experience of African American communities, or the most superficial understanding of the social/cultural/historical context of Blues I think are interacting with African

American cultural values when they attempt to play Blues in a style fashioned after African American culture), as professionals providing a service requested by an employer, as people expressing themselves through performance. Blues musicians don't get swallowed up, sold out, or plowed over by dominating trends in commercial/economic/racial power structures of the scene, just as they are not subsumed by some single definition of what Blues or an ethnic identity is.

"I try to show my students the African American musical elements and values that shape Blues, R&B, Rap, and Rock in all its forms. I try to show the value of identifying African American cultural elements that mainstream America may not acknowledge and show how asserting the cultural identity or contributions of African American cultural things does not mean that non-African Americans are excluded as a result." Susan cited these reasons why some players play for little or no money:

> 1.) They love Blues music, and performing more than some other profession that might provide a steadier living.

> 2.) They have a day job that helps with the bills.

> 3.) The system keeps going this way.

The Upside Down Pyramid Syndrome

Do Caucasian agents, managers, and lawyers outlive the Black artists they represent? Maybe not, but it sure seems like it. I've seen several cases where Black entertainers have started out in control and on top of their business and a couple of major shows and recording projects later they appear to be working for the very "support" group (or at least *they* think they do) that once supported them. What's up with that? How do we fall into that trap? Why do we fall into that trap? Is it because many of us Blacks believe:

a. Black agents and managers will rip us off.

b. Blacks don't have the connections that White folks do.

c. Blacks entertainers are held in higher esteem and seem more credible when represented by Whites.

Whatever the case, many of us Black musicians, athletes, actors, entertainers and artists of all kinds seem to fall prey to what I call *the Upside Down Pyramid Syndrome* more often than not. What is this syndrome? Does it only apply to Blacks in the fields of entertainment, or is its reach far greater? If so, how great?

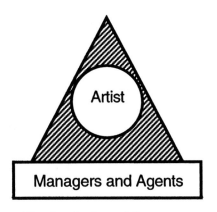

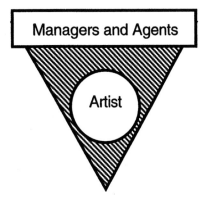

The beginning of the career   The end of the career

This section is very personal because it's grounded in conversations many of us as professional performers (Black, White, and others) continually have. One day I was asked to produce a compilation CD inspired by a *Chicago Tribune Magazine* article written by Howard Reich on Sunday, December 27, 1998, of which I was one of the featured artists spotlighted. By the middle of the conversation it was obvious that the *cat* in charge of this project was not used to dealing with Black Bluesmen as businessmen. Needless to say, the deal didn't go down. Consciousness of the Upside Down Pyramid saved me from being ripped off.

Jeff Todd Titon wrote in Early Downhome Blues: "The record companies were among the first White American institutions to try to sell Black Americans a product they could refuse to buy. Their advertising, while not surprisingly incorporating deep-seated racism, also revealed careful attempts to understand Black people and their music. It exhibited the ambivalent feelings, ambiguous symbols, and contradictory activities, which White Americans continue until this day. Because advertising is an attempt to create and sustain a community of consumers based upon an image of who they are who they should like to become, advertisements are a particularly rich source of information about how people are perceived and the directions in which they are pushed."

Professor Caleb Dube from Northwestern University said, "My assumption is that the constraints, opportunities, and strategies of survival that musicians experience and devise as workers are generated by the tension between conflicting roles. The tension is primarily generated by the commoditization of music making.

"Struggling [Black] Blues musicians find themselves torn in between artistic commitment, and making good money to enable them to make a decent living. Most musicians who consider themselves as having been called by higher spiritual forces to be performers have a higher artistic aim than money, yet they expect to be paid for their work. However, these concerns are not always compatible with one another."

It sounds like a broken record, but at times it seems as if everyone gets paid but the Bluesman and woman. They are often under paid, over worked, and under appreciated. For a lifetime, many run through mazes and jump hurdles in search of fame, fortune, recognition, and most importantly, understanding.

Who's supporting what?

On Saturday, September 3, 1988, I asked my friend, Ron Robertson, about sharing his thoughts on young African Americans supporting the Blues he said, "It's just a matter of getting the word out there and making it more accessible to the general Black public. The best example of that is the White British musicians who heard the Blues many years ago and took it and incorporated it into their music. They were able to win over the White audiences, whereas, the Black audiences really haven't been won over yet. It just isn't out there for them to hear. "Most modern music is an involvement of the early Blues, the Delta Blues, that they turned into Rock & Roll and Bebop. It's that art form our ancestors brought over on the slave ships." Dr. Asa Hilliard said, "If I am clothed in my right mind then I will know who I am, and I can't leave pieces of me behind because I can't be coherent if I don't have it all."

John Primer, former rhythm guitar player for Muddy Waters, said, "It's not out there. Get it out there, and I'm sure they'll like it. The young Blacks have come a long way. They didn't seem to like the Blues at first because they have always liked Disco and Rock & Roll and stuff like that. Now the younger ones are liking the Blues. I've liked the Blues all of my life and came up with it while growing up in Mississippi. It was something to love and something that you could make money at if you could play it."

Nelson George wrote in his book the <u>Death of Rhythm & Blues</u>: "The record industry began as a stepchild of the sheet-music business, since popular tunes originally were consumed primarily through the sale of sheet music. When newspapers labeled ragtime *'vulgar, filthy, and suggestive'* because of its vibrant, sexual dance ability, the Black elite, who were highly sensitive to what Whites thought of them, agreed, implying that such overt displays of the *'African spirit'* hindered the advancement of the race."

In a 1990 Ebony Magazine article by Charles Whitaker entitled "Are Blacks Giving the Blues Away?" John Lee Hooker was quoted as saying, "Black people today don't seem that interested in the Blues. They want to get away from it. They think the Blues is a downer, something left over from slavery times." The article also addressed the closet fans. In that article Etta James said, "They're the same people who will have a Saturday night fish fry, invite their mama over, play all the B.B. King, T-Bone Walker and Howlin' Wolf that they can get their hands on, but shut all the doors and windows up tight cause they don't want anybody to know."

Bluesologist Ralph Metcalfe, Jr. said, "The reason we [Blacks] shy away from the Blues is because of our self-hatred. We hate ourselves. We worship the White man's gods more so than being concerned with our own heritage and origins. The Blues musicians in the beginning where the traveling minstrels. Black educators do not teach this in school because they have not been trained themselves. We have to fight that self-hatred. When I was [an undergraduate student] at Columbia University, I went to the music department [and] it was filled with Brahms, Beethoven, and Bach instead of [Muddy] Waters, [Howlin'] Wolf, and [Junior] Wells. That's racist! The Blues is the Classical music of Black people. The fact is that the young *cuties* are into Disco and Rap music. Young Black folks have their tastes dictated to them by an industry that is not in control by those with their best interest at heart, but by somebody who doesn't."

"Additionally," Blueswoman Sydney Ellis said, "Blues is an Afro-American folk art. It has only one place of origin, both geographically and culturally. Everything else is just something mimicking it. Because of over commercialization there are a lot of people who are trying to make a name for themselves on the back of Blues, and, unfortunately, it takes away from the folk art. This is not to say that one has to be Black in order to be authentic or good at it. It's just that culturally, this folk art is a part of the Afro-American heritage. It is not normally associated with other cultural histories. It is like the difference between speaking in your native language and a second language. It is easy to qualify what I am trying to say this way. There is no way to separate this folk art from the Afro-American history. I know a lot of Afro-Americans who do not like Blues, [they] don't sing it, don't play it, can t even relate to it, but at the same time they know it's part of their history."

Chicago Blueswoman Barbara LeShoure said, "Black people consider Blues to be slave music; they don't want to be identified as slaves. I, don't understand that because I'm still in slavery. You can't get around it. You see, the thing about it is that they don't want to be reminded, but you have to face reality. I ain't gonna never ignore it, nor am I gonna be ripped off of my music because that's another insult. I've been a Blues singer all of my life. I went to work and they took a White woman over me and tried to make her a star. That's the highest insult in the world. You know I'm not having that—to take a Black cultural music that they think you are not aware of?"

Professor Sterling D. Plumpp from the University of Illinois at Chicago grew up picking cotton and doing farm chores in Mississippi during the 1940s. He said, "It had been known as a plantation in a tenant situation where the land had been plotted out to different families. My grandfather lived his entire seventy-four years in that situation, and I lived fifteen years of my life in that kind of a relationship. Music would be blaring in the late hours of the night from Nashville, Tennessee and Del Rio, Texas. And I heard crude attempts by my uncles trying to sing the Blues as they plowed [the fields] or chopped wood, but the entire experience of the rural South is an oral experience. The Blues is a great deal of that experience sung lyrically to a highly rhythmical kind of music.

"It was a segregated market and it was the late 1940s in the later stages of my childhood. That was the music that I heard. If you have a segregated audience there is no need to change the music to get an audience." He said that when Chuck Berry and Bo Diddley up-tempoed Blues they created Rock & Roll and Rhythm & Blues, and that's when White audiences became "fascinated and attracted to that part of the Blues." The Godfather of Blues poetry feels like the beneficiaries of these works are those he calls the *pretenders to the throne.*

He said, "When they began to play and market that product [White Blues bands] that was an extension of the Blues. The Blues was the way [Black] people told their stories, and it was also the way that they faced the realities of their lives. And I think it has remained that; White America has never had any need to give African Americans credit for any of the genius or made them wealthy for producing such genius. Very few of the people who created Jazz were ever very wealthy. Duke Ellington never made the money that he deserved to make nor did Charlie Parker, John Coltrane, or Thelonious Monk. I expect *the pretenders to the throne* to make all of the money because that's how racism works.

"It was a Black boy sitting at the feet of another Black boy; it was Muddy Waters sitting at the feet of Charley Patton that gives you the Blues, and Junior Wells sitting at the feet of Muddy Waters [that] gives you the Blues. There is no White musician in the Blues who has achieved the stature in the Blues that Muddy Waters has achieved. To make some White boys [the Beatles] from Liverpool, England the inheritors of the Blues is a good public relations job. I think their music was very authentic, but I just don't think it was Blues. Black musicians are not treated as the geniuses they are. The fact is that a Black kid who follows in the tradition of Muddy Waters will never be as important as a White boy who steals from Muddy like the Rolling Stones.

"The thesis behind White America is that you can only be important if somebody White says so. If you are Black and you play Blues from now until the end of eternity, and you sit at the feet of Muddy Waters from the time you are two until the time you are ten, it is not as important as if you are a White boy taking Muddy and playing with him in London. That's a racist theory. That's what society promotes. If I don't have an institution to exist in then I become part clown then the ability that I [the artist] once had I lose. My perception is that the White, Yuppie Lincoln Park audience tends to like high-energy music. They think that Blues should show some sort of relationship to Rock & Roll. Therefore, a great deal of potentially significant Black Blues musicians distort what the music is about to please that audience."

Steve Cushing of WBEZ had this comment: "There came a time when White people started listening to Blues. We have to face the fact that Blues is not going to be the way we've known it. I don't think you are going to get people to play the Blues as we've known it. When Big Bill [Broonzy], Sonny Boy [Williamson], and Big Maceo hit the end of their era, at the end of the '40s, there was nothing that really brought them back. It was just the sign of the times. I think we've just got to get used to the idea that that's the way Blues is going to be from now on, for better or worse."

Sterling D. Plumpp feels that when our ancestors sang field hollers they were not "setting out to entertain White folks." He said, "They stole all that stuff on Tin Pan Alley, and an Afro-American's writings will never be as important as William Faulkner writing about Black America. There is a long tradition of having others portray Afro-Americans and it is accepted as being more valid than Afro-American writers writing about themselves. The only thing that needs to be done is for Blacks to develop first rate Blues clubs on the South side of Chicago; try to develop a better pay scale, and try to get as many young Blacks interested in playing the music the way it was originated."

When asked about Whites recognizing their Black mentors Plumpp said, "If they gave proper recognition Buddy Guy would be bigger in music than Eric Clapton. He's not."

Below is a chart of Dr. Ronald Myers' philosophy on the four types of musicians.

The Innovator	has no boundaries as a musician
The Propagator	learns from, but does imitate the innovator
The Imitator	is a copy cat with very little originality
The Instigator	promotes the music for the sole purpose of economic gain

THREE
Influences

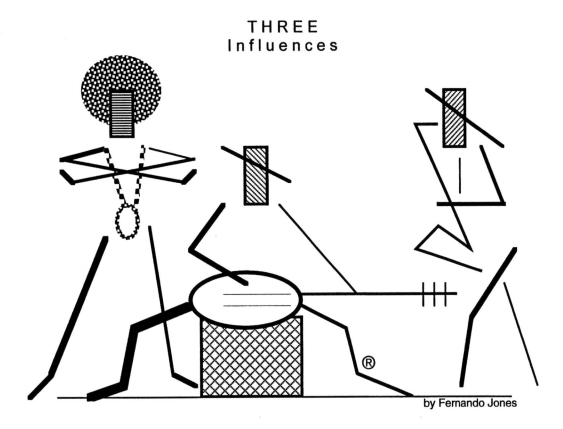

by Fernando Jones

This section is going to talk about the influences that the Blues has had on other styles of music and artistic forms of expression.

On Jazz

Leroi Jones wrote in <u>Blues People</u>: "The Blues is the parent of all legitimate Jazz, and it is impossible to say exactly how old Blues is—certainly no older than the presence of Negroes in the United States. It is a Native American music, the product of Black people in this country; or to put it more exactly the way I have come to think about it, Blues could not exist if the African captives had not become American captives."

Most of us fans know that Jazz was born in Louisiana, but don't know where the name came from, or how the title came about. Well, it's my understanding that Jazz was first called *Jass* in the late 1800s to describe the music being played by Black musicians in whore houses. Oddly enough, the musicians were calling what they were playing the Blues. Seeing that some White folks in those days had very little regard for Black folks—that music was called "Jack-ass" Music.

Trumpet player Pevin Everett (apprentice of Wynton Marsalis) said, "It came from the word *Jizz,* and in the 1800s, *Jizz Joints* were places that hookers, and tramps, and that type of thing would go. And to take the edge off of the word 'Jizz' they just put an 'a' in there and made it Jazz. And Jazz itself transpired from that word. So, therefore, you had a 'low class' form of music given to the 'lower class' man, and that's how the word Jazz came to be."

Dr. Frank Adams said, "After playing both Blues and Jazz, there's no difference. And I think any musician who has had experience in playing them both will give you the same answer. The Blues is that which gave birth to Jazz. We start with a basic twelve bar form, and we talk about form in a music like AAB, or AAA. We come with the Blues form and we learn to play the Blues, and there are certain inflections in the Blues, certain accents, certain emphasis on certain notes and meters in Jazz that can only come from the Blues. So, there might be some stylistic thing that we do, but basically they are the same, and I recommend to any person who attempts to play Jazz to really study the Blues and learn how to play the Blues. In fact, I'm giving the advice of people like Charlie Parker, John Coltrane, all those who came up playing the Blues. In fact, if you hear of a Jazz solo that does not have any Blues inflections in it I'd like to hear about it.

"The experience of playing with Duke Ellington was the greatest experience of my life. I would say that so far as the Blues is concerned. He held the Blues in the highest respect, and most of his compositions were proud portrayals of the Blues. Ellington was proud to be a Blues player, really, and if you ever got into a circle of people who knew him, or were in this circle, praise was always given to the Blues. In fact, when it was called 'Jazz' as you know if you look into the history of Ellington, he never accepted the word 'Jazz' and didn't think that music should be categorized as Jazz, but he accepted the word Blues as a descriptor. He would never call his compositions—let's say *Sophisticated Lady* or *Mood Indigo* Jazz music.

"When Ellington used a twelve bar extended twelve bar line as Blues, he always gave credit to the Blues players. In fact, when he constructed his band he had New Orleans Blues players like Sydney Bechét to form the greatest band in the world. And never in all the years I knew Ellington, and before and after, if you look at the personnel in his band he never had any players other than players with a Blues background. The first thing that he would tell you to do in playing with his band would be, if you played a solo, was [to] create and tell a story. That's what the Blues has always done."

Baptist preacher, medical doctor, and professional Jazz piano player Ronald Myers was mentored by Jimmy Cheatham, John Coltrane's trombone player. Ron now resides in Tschula, Mississippi. "Jazz and Blues, in my opinion, have the same roots. I believe it all came out of an expression from the heart of the kidnapped African in America and what he suffered. Through *his* oppression *he* was able to take the drum and begin to express the deep sorrow of *his* experience. You have to understand that Jazz, in my opinion, is nothing but a sophisticated form of the Blues. It's just a more intricate way of expressing the Blues. Jazz is African American Classical music. It is a music that is unique to the experience of the kidnapped African slave in America. Jazz was unique because it was a form of *Black talk.*"

Jazz aficionado Troy Norman said: "The emphasis of Blues is more vocal than Jazz. Jazz has, over the course of its existence, developed instrumentally more than vocally. There are Jazz vocalists, there always have been, but the musical emphasis has been on the development of individual instruments and technique on the instrument the musician is playing. The instruments serve more as a mood for the context in which the vocalist sings. The Blues has always been a major part of the Jazz vocabulary. Even today many of the younger people are finding that a functional appreciation of the Blues is necessary to evolve the music further." Felton Crews (former bass player for Miles Davis) said, "Miles would always put a Blues song up front in the concert. It was like he was trying to catch the band on fire because that was the one song everyone could relate to."

"Jazz started out as marching band music," Dr. Ronald Myers said, "using brass instruments, as well as drums. Pioneers such as Buddy Bolden, Jelly Roll Morton, and Joe 'King' Oliver (Louis Armstrong's mentor) were some of the more important figures in early Jazz. The Blues served as a template for Jazz improvisation. King Oliver did not want his music recorded because he felt his soul would be trapped in that recording."

Writer Rahsaan Morris from the *Jazz Institute Newsletter* said, "When you talk about the major influence of the Blues on Jazz the writers, [and] composers all of them have a Blues background. When you get off into the *Cool Period of Jazz* with Miles Davis, Jerry Mulligan, and Gil Evans—once again there is *this* reference in all of their music. Cool music was really the up tempo Bebop slowed down. They were tired of Swing and the Beboppers were trying to form their own language of music.

"Even to this day Wynton Marsalis and Marcus Roberts will tell you [that] Blues is at the root of what they do, if you take into account that the genesis of this [music] is actually New Orleans with Louis Armstrong and Bix Beiderbecke. These musicians took Blues riffs and elongated them. They used the twelve bar and 16 bar Blues for their tune construction in Jazz. Now, we jump ahead and go from Louis Armstrong to somebody as important as Duke Ellington. He and Billy Strayhorn would use Blues construction when they orchestrated their tunes from the '30s on up. Now you jump from Duke Ellington to somebody like Charlie Parker, Thelonius Monk, and Dizzy Gillespie who invented Bebop. They still used Blues instrumentation, and by that I mean guitar, bass, and drums as a rhythm section, and then they'd have a melody instrument over the top, but the tunes they'd play even though they were fast and up tempo were constructed in sixteen bar form. And what is that but Blues construction?" Here is a song that was written and produced by yours truly called *It's Rainin' Again*. It, too, is an example of the Blues and Jazz as one.

> *It's rainin' again and I feel like I'm born to lose.*
> *Well, it's rainin' again and I feel like I'm born to lose.*
> *If I get wet enough it'll wash away my mood.*
>
> *Sometimes I feel like weepin', but only moans'll come. (2x)*
> *I feel like the moon being destroyed by the sun.*
>
> *Some say I'm a diamond. Others say I'm a precious jewel. (2x)*
> *I am what I am and I'm still in love with you. (2x)*

On Rap

Rap music, in particular, has been part of the African community and culture for as long as people have used words to communicate. The foundation of what we today call "Rap" can be traced all the way back to Africa to a time when our forefathers were just nameless, faceless 'hep' poets talkin' tribal *jive*. We have always talked and walked with some sort of *groove*. It's kind of like shooting pool and puttin' a little English (or *Ang-glish* as we call it) on the cue ball. Dig? Rap is not necessarily about rhyming, it's about communicating. Besides, people of African decent have always had their own way of *doin' thangs*.

Not since the birth of Rock & Roll in the early '50s has one music form reshaped the music industry so much. Rap and Hip-hop grooves have even crossed over into Country & Western music influencing artists such as Neal McCoy and Shania Twain.

Admittedly, when I heard *Rappers Delight* by the Sugar Hill Gang (I was in 7th or 8th grade) that was the coolest tune I'd ever heard. Who would have ever thought Rap would still be goin' strong? Some of the things those Rappers have come up with using sampled loops of pre-recorded songs and drum machines have blown my mind. I'm not ready to trade in my Telecaster for a turntable, but I've got to give 'em their props just the same.

By the 1990s, the millions of dollars generated from record sales, concerts, merchandising, and even movies featuring Rap artist far outweighed the negative publicity that once surrounded the stereotypical images of the hardcore Rappers keepin' it real.

These "musical ambassadors of the ghetto," as Nova Parham calls them, are making a dent in the world economy. Since production costs are nominal and the returns have consistently been astronomical, those who once loathed it have now embraced it . . . millions of dollars later. In defense of Hip-hop, Rap, and the urban youth, this music is no more controversial today than Rock & Roll was in the '50s. And the Blues is the center of both art forms.

Could the negative responses towards this music have something to do with the fact that this art form is dominated by young, aggressive Blacks from the inner city? Today in America, Black entertainment (music, movies, clothing lines, etcetera) is a very profitable export; when you think of Black music, today, Hip-hop and Rap probably come to mind. However, I do not condone the violence or hate filled words passed off as "Black Rage" and *keepin' it real* by some of its practitioners. On the other hand, I'm mature enough to know that not all of Rap and Hip-hop is vulgar. Back in the day (the late '70s), Rap was either braggadocios and/or uplifting. Not violent just conscious. Kelvin "Rappn Tate Da Great" says, "If it was not for R&B Rap music would not have been in existence today. It was Blues that helped Rap artists express themselves with more clarity and identity, and show freedom of expression. After all, the Blues is a Heavenly sent rainbow covenant."

Check this out, I was on a Southwest airplane sitting next to a young lady named Nova Parham on Sunday, March 1,1998. We were flying from Los Angeles to Chicago. She used to co-manage a Rap group called the Racc Pacc. She told me that Suge Knight of Death Row Records was interested in signing her group to his label, but the lead Rapper was shot to death and that kept the deal from happening. So I asked her about the attraction and fascination Black inner city youths seem to have with Rap and Nova said, "It's a way out for our

Black men today. You know what I mean? I'd say that nine out of ten Rappers don't have a college degree, [but] you don't have to have a college degree to do this. You can just share your life story and become an overnight success. It's like the Lord just sent Black men a way to make it. It's a sign of the times, period."

Who cares about the nappy headed four hundred year old Black boys
That played with pyramid rocks because there were no toys?
What about the Vaseline faced little girls taught not to dream
While listening to recapitulated sounds of apocalyptic screams?
Therefore, never knowing the even flow and balance
Life experiences bring.

On Comedy

Blacks have often used humor to stimulate and sustain their audiences. Comedy is a form of entertainment that you may not have normally associated with the Blues. For generations comedians such as Amos & Andy, Bill Cosby, Redd Foxx, Moms Mabley, Pig Meat Markham, and Richard Pryor have guided us through the lives and times of Black folks, in Black neighborhoods, in Black households, in Black situations through humor. The Blues encompasses the Diaspora of Black artistic expression in the United States of America.

What is it that makes us laugh? Is it the rhythm? Could it be the delivery of the punch line? The diction? Could it be the mere appearance of the comic itself? From *playing the dozens* to plain ole signifying, the thing that makes us laugh is the familiarity beneath it all. We've all got either an aunt, uncle, cousin, or parent who drinks too much on Friday night, curses everyone out at the fish fry at Big Mama's house on Saturday night, and gets up and goes to the church house on Sunday only to point fingers at everybody else. That's funny because we are able to laugh at ourselves then move on.

Comedian Carl Wright, who also wrote Muddy Waters' *She's into Somethin',* said, "Comedy is a present reality. Laughter frees the mind to be nice to people. It lessens the violent thoughts." Comedy is cathartic. I believe it takes the place of Black folks going to the psychiatrist. We use comedy as forms of social commentary everyday in our culture. If comedy wasn't filled with the truth it wouldn't be funny to any of us.

The more you laugh, the less you cry. From an African American perspective, comedy allows us an opportunity to laugh at things that are embarrassing without being too embarrassed. In our culture, comedy helps us deal with things as diverse and complex as relationships, death, depression, envy, jealousy, misery, poverty, and even sexual frustrations. And guess what, comedy gets us through all of that jive without a single visit to the psychiatrist's office. Check this out, comedy has saved many, many, many people of all colors and creeds millions of dollars in therapy.

Here's a line from the Play Blues for Jesus written by Carl Vanoy and yours truly. There are five laws that every Bluesman must abide by:
    5.) Be on time.
    4.) Drive a Cadillac.
    3.) Look as good as you sound.
    2.) Your woman must have all of her teeth even if they're in a case.
    1.) You must have a lid on at all times.

On Theater

To get some feedback on how much the Blues has influenced theater in Black America I went to the ETA Creative Arts Foundation and talked to Dr. Abena Joan Brown. She said, "Well, I think the Blues has influenced every major art form in the United States of America. The Blues [and] Spirituals, along with Gospel and all of its derivatives, actually, are America's music. The Blues is a way to tell a story. Theater is based on a story. It's from that simplistic response one can see that story telling is story telling, and it comes in many different forms, and in many different venues. But for music, particularly the Blues and theater, the telling of stories, which accurately and validly depict our experience and our aspiration, go hand-and-hand. They're the same.

"Many people, playwrights, have written plays which have a Blues motif using the music as a launching pad for the beat, and the syncopation and staccato of the words. August Wilson has been particularly known in recent times with that, but earlier on Langston Hughes did the same thing. Jimmy [James] Baldwin did the same thing using Gospel [music], which, I think, is the sister to the Blues. So it's the same family. It's another way to express; to tell our story. One understands the cultural paradigm, and culture is that vehicle which drives all people in terms of their traditions, their values, their aspirations, their lifestyle, and their norms.

"That's why even when we go to the movies, we talk back. We talk to the movie screen. Many of us, if not most, talk to the television screen [and] comment upon what's going on. Another thing I would say about the music is that if we recognize who we are and what we bring to the cultural scene in the United States of America, and the world, then we would understand why product commercials are backed up by our music. We will understand that wherever we travel in the world that we have influenced the artistic forms of every country in the world. Am I making sense? We're the ones. In the early days of theater, Black companies did mostly White plays. So it's kind of a reverse experience. Where we moved in the '60s and '70s, and with the rising consciousness now in the '90s, is to tell our story in the first voice as we know it, and experience it rather than having others tell our story to perpetuate the stereotypes which have historically been put out there about who we are.

"So it's a different kind of struggle. The struggle has been: One, to get Black people to understand that we have a story that is uniquely ours, and only we can tell it. Two, advancing our own traditional lifestyles and values that we hold so that we can have call-and-response when we sit in the theaters and say, 'I know these people [because] these people are me,' rather than making that stretch to identify with the stories of others. And at the same time we must develop strategies and institutions where our stories can be told because a good story is a good story, and a universal story. But the universality of good stories are not just designated to one group of people. There are many cultures in the world and all of them have authenticity and validity.

"We are entitled to our own world view which differs from the world view of others. I would say the same is true of the Spanish speaking story and all of its nuances. The same is true of the Asian story and its cultural nuances. And the same is true of the African story. That's what the struggle is about right now. That's what its about which differs from the music. The music is more direct As a function of racism, many groups of people think that our story couldn't possibly be their story, but that's a function of racism, and that's not our work to undo. Our work is to tell our story for ourselves, to ourselves, by ourselves for the affirmation of ourselves."

Runako Jahi, Artistic Director at the ETA Creative Arts Foundation, said, "The theater has always been influenced by the culture of the Blues because the Blues is made of the elements that are essential to good theater. Passion, lust, greed, drive, love, disappointment, heartache—[are] the *feelings* we all share as humans. That is why the Blues has never faded and never will.

"The Blues is something everybody gets. From the rich to the poor, beneath the surface, the Blues always lingers. You can't run from the Blues. We are happiness, and we are the Blues. Many great works of art, from the cinema to dance, to paintings and poetry, the essence of the Blues always makes its presence known. It bears the pulse of all human emotion—of all of the arts disciplines.

"I wouldn't say that the Blues appeals to all theater goers. Many people prefer other kinds of music: Gospel, Hip-hop, Jazz, Classical, R&B, Folk, etc. Even though I personally like certain Blues songs, my soul element is Jazz, but that's me. Black people know that the Blues is ours. It's our story. It's not always sad and down. It is as jubilant in its own way as our revered Gospel music.

"In the theater, the Bluesman is represented as the realist. No frills [just] the real thing. Nothing is covered up. It's all right there, raw and right between the eyes. Certain people can take that kind of total honesty, but others can't. What makes the Bluesman significant is that all he can do is tell it like it is."

Co-writer and producer, Carl Vanoy, of the Chicago based play *Blues For Jesus* said, "There's an excitement in the Blues. The people are truthful. They speak their minds, and they let out all of their emotions. The Blues is whatever you are feeling at the time. That's my perception. If you're feelin happy you have happy Blues [and] you've got sad Blues. It's your presence in life."

On Film

David "D.P." Carlson said, "Most of my films have been narratives, and I just started work in documentary film. And being that Chicago is my hometown, I felt a certain attachment to the material. I'm a firm believer that you should try something new with every film you direct. And for me, the process of submerging myself into the Blues scene allowed me to gain a new found respect for a music and a people that I had yet to explore."

On Commercial and Industrial Products

In addition to the countless movies that have featured Blues based music here are some everyday products that have been promoted by using Blues songs, too (within the last five years): All (detergent), Budweiser and Coors (beer), *Chicago Tribune* (newspaper), Pepsi Cola and Diet Coca~Cola (soft drinks), Fisher-Price (toys), Porsche and Jaguar (automobiles), Kraft (macaroni & cheese), Esteé Lauder (perfume), Levi's (blue jeans), M&M's (candy), McDonald's (hamburgers),

Fernando Jones

TGI Frdays (restaurant), Viagra (medicine), Hanes (underwear), and Vitner's (potato chips).

"They've resurrected," Dr. Abena Joan Brown said, "Billie Holiday [and] Dinah Washington, Chuck Berry, James Brown—they all now have given the back-beat to commercials to sell products. Right? They know when that beat comes on people listen. [They] can't help but listen. [They] can't escape it. It gives body and substance to the words. We just have to be careful that our music is not co-opted and used for the economic advancement of others as opposed to ourselves." Kofi Moyo, co-founder of Real Men Cook said, "The Blues is the baseline and foundation that keeps the other things together."

As you watch TV or listen to the radio this week, list products that have Blues based music or thematic content in them.

Product	Date	Time

FOUR
The Importance of the Blues
From a sociological & historical perspective with a focus on the future:
Showcasing African American educators, musicians, and Blues Kids

by Fernando Jones

Though this music and culture were not meant to be institutionalized, or intellectualized, this section will introduce you to some of the Blues' biggest and brightest supporters from all across America. These fantastic folks come from all walks of African American life, and they will share their most heart felt moments with you. At this time I'd like introduce you to these world class educators, musicians, college students, and even children from my very own Blues Kids of America program. Pour yourself a cup or glass of your favorite "favorite" and enjoy the ride. I mean *the read.* ☺

Dr. Charles D. Moody, Sr.
National Alliance of Black School Educators, Founder
Vice Provost Emeritus, University of Michigan

First of all, I want to say [that] the Blues is my favorite! I've never been ashamed of it. I've always loved them. It brings back memories when I was a little boy growin' up in Louisiana going to those fish fries, and seeing a lot of people. It tells a story of us and our struggle. It also gives us hope. I just get excited when someone starts asking me about the Blues. In fact, a few months ago when my friend, Lee Martin, was recuperating from surgery, I went over and brought all my Blues records and tapes, and we sat, and we listened, and we reminisced. We thought about the kinds of common experiences we had had although we grew up in different places and at different times, but we had experiences that were common. And the Blues was the thing that ran through those kinds of experiences that we had.

The Blues really tells our story. It talks about the hard times, the good times we've had and the things we've done to make it. I think the thing that is most distressing and disheartening, to me, is to see the number of African Americans who get some alphabets behind their name who don't want to listen to the Blues and don't want to be affiliated with the Blues. And [then) you go to Blues concerts and 99% of the people there are White, and they have taken the Blues and pretty soon it will be their creation.

I think our [Black] kids need to know so they can be proud of the fact that [their] people did overcome some of these kinds of things. I think it's very critical that the Blues be seen for what it really is, and that is . . . this is an original piece of American music. People are always talkin' about Jazz and things, but when you think about it when the slaves were in the fields they were singin' the Blues. They weren't playin' no Jazz. So I think that's very critical for people to know that and understand that. If people can free themselves of being scared to talk about the Blues, or deal with the Blues in mixed company, or amongst themselves they'll be all right.

Dr. Barbara Sizemore
Legendary Educator, Chicago

I think the real purpose of the Blues, sociologically, for African American people is that it tells them a lot about the history of the people especially during the period that followed the first Reconstruction beginning in 1875/1876 to the present. During that time, African Americans were deeply disappointed because the Reconstruction effort didn't work, and the 13th, 14th and 15th Amendments were negated by the Black Code laws that were passed by the Reconstruction government(s) of the previous Confederate States. And together with that effect on their lives, the Blues was an outlet [and] a way to record what was happening to them and how they felt about it. And I think that continues.

Culture is the sum total of artifacts that any group accumulates in its struggles for survival and autonomy, and African Americans are no different from any other group. They are still struggling. The first struggle, of course, for survival is just that you can stay alive and carry out nature's purpose, which is reproduction of the species. And then of course, in order to survive you have to preserve the group. That is, be sure that every member of the group keeps his or her body in strong enough physical health and then to take care of the progeny.

Culturally, in the sum total of artifacts, the Blues are an artifact that the group has accumulated in this struggle and it's an intricate part of that struggle. So I think it's crucial that it be taught [in schools].

Dr. Lily Golden
Professor of African American Studies at Chicago State University

I lived in Uzbekistan and in Russia, and these countries don't have things like Blues or Gospel music, but they have Jazz. Blues is full of folk music, and it developed as an answer to those social conditions of which only Blacks lived. That's why the Blues is in a very specific context.

When I came to the United States, I was expecting to hear Black music from morning to evening. I found several radio stations, but only a few played Gospel and Blues. Blues is [the] Classical music of Black people.

Dr. Nora Martin
Professor at Eastern Michigan University, Psychologist

The Blues is important to me because I like what it represents in my African American heritage. And it's one thing that sure, we want to spread, but it still has its roots in our heritage. I'm always struck by the intelligence behind it. Many people overlook that, but when you think of the lyrics and how they're put together it takes a lot of intelligence and creativity to come up with that.

A soulful kind of mood, it can put you into, and that gets at this whole psychological world-being even when the Blues is being blue still can be uplifting. When you think of Blues and the very shades of blue, it can be as deep as Blues and it can still make you hum. It can make you kind of lay back and reflect, and certainly relax, too. It really can, and more than anything else, it makes you think because you start to relate to the lyrics of the story behind the lyrics.

Dr. Bobbiette Turner
Chicago Public School Administrator

The Blues is man's way if relating his or her everyday experiences and dreams in a style that is unique to the African American culture. To me, the Blues is the symphonic poetry of a people which relates our struggles, and self-concepts that we projected, and in certain instances we continue to project some of these concepts. The relationship of the Blues to my existence is historical. The Blues is part of my history, my life, and my father's life.

It is important that we of African American decent study and/or teach this art because it is *art*. It is part of our musical foundation, and our historical growth from slavery to the modern age. Many young people do not know what the Blues is about and, therefore, an essential part of their total picture is fragmented or misshapen.

It is the responsibility of African American, Asian American, and European Americans all to have music which reflects their culture. We have music and it must not be shoved aside. Old and new artists must come together and pass on the Blues tradition and let it flow through the ears of our young people. The Blues should point our children toward success and a higher sense of self-worth. Remember all of the Blues is not *blue*.

Dr. Lee Martin
Psychologist, Ann Arbor, Michigan

As an African American male, an extremely critical part of my heritage is music. Within the context of music I have numerous loves. One that always surfaces is Blues. Blues to me presents a way of life and a deep appreciation for our sense of being, our sense of existence. Many of the trials that we've experienced, living here in America, is reflected in the Blues. It also deals with those tribulations that we've experienced, It becomes a sobering way of soothing those feelings as part of this whole entire process. Its more like a catharsis, it's one of releasing these feelings. But also one of developing a keen sense of appreciation for both the music and the lyric that emanates from the Blues.

One of the great traditions that Africans Americans have been credited for is the field of music. I think if we tend to let one of our contributions be mainstreamed it certainly further takes away from our identity as a people. I think when we look at it, all people who reside here in the United States, and throughout the world they each make unique contributions. For African Americans, I think this is important that we can look back and reflect. This is an art form that truly represents all of us, and we must maintain those pieces of identity of culture, which truly represents an identity of life.

As African Americans what has happened [is that] we've been severed in many ways from our familial environment from our roots, from our ancestors. We have given over to mainstream culture and mainstream way of life. Instead of maintaining that strong family unity that we had, we tended to rely more over, in terms of mass culture taking over the responsibility for rearing us, and what is proper, and what really belongs to us as a people.

From a psychological standpoint, this is the basis of mental health—one having a true sense of identity. When we tend to deny this and look to others then we look for others to validate our existence. So we must maintain those art forms and those cultural ways that are unique to African Americans. It becomes a source of strength and becomes the propelling force that's going to keep us being quite competitive along with a sense of identity.

Dr. Ernest Holloway
Langston University, President

We've seen a lot of people who've tried to imitate the Blues, and they're even trying to sing it. The Blues grew out of a life of living. You can't sing the Blues if you haven't experienced the Blues, and I think that's the future.

On my campus, even as a University, we have a segment focusing on the Blues. Our people in our music department take time to talk about and teach students majoring in music all phases in music.

Dr. Deborah Hammond
Chicago Public School Administrator

I've always liked the Blues because it always told a story. While some of the stories were not so positive, the Blues always had a happy ending. I can remember somebody saying how the Blues develops from a mood. It's the beat, the story, the repetition that makes the Blues stand out from all the other music.

The Blues has gotten Black people through many troubled times. We can go back to the times of slavery when it was just something that Black folks shared. We know that there are now White people who get paid for playing the Blues, and actually that's okay because that means that they've learned

41

something from the Black population. They realized that the Black culture had something they could learn and make money from.

From a social aspect, I believe it's a segment of music that Black people share and that it's something we can call our own. While other races play the Blues, the feeling or "soul" is seldom duplicated. Economically, I think that the Black community has gotten shafted because of economical drawbacks. I know that all of the money made from the Blues did not make it into the hands of its creators. We know that there are some Black musicians who have written many songs who have recorded those songs, and are now driving cabs because their music was sold on the "black" market.

Dr. Asa Hilliard
Egyptologist and Professor, Georgia State University

I think the best way I can express it [the Blues] is that somewhere around 1979 or so, a friend of mine was working with me on some history we were doing. I was doing a lecture on African History, Ancient Kemet History, and so she asked, "If you had your dream for a place to present this, what would your best wish be if you had somebody to present with you?" And I thought about it for a long time. I think she was asking it because she thought I was gonna say another historian, and I said the best thing that would make me the happiest is if I could present this with Bobby Bland. So she did arrange an actual presentation, and Bobby and I presented in the same audience. One of the roots of that whole experience, if we understand it, is manifested in the Blues.

When I'm reaching for something deep then almost always is gonna be some Gospel or Blues song. That will be the thing that will create the environment, and then that makes everything else more whole. So from a spiritual side, that's what that means.

From the historical and cultural side, it's our own music. The fact that a lot of White musicians are now very good at the Blues doesn't change that one bit. That music is strictly African music created in the African community to express African meanings, intent, feeling, and what have you. Most of us in my generation were raised on that. You know? I, in Texas, and some of my other friends in other places, but because we tend to try and understand ourselves by looking at the pieces we tend to leave out some of the most important pieces.

All you have to do is go, right now, in some of those old villages anywhere on the West African coast, in particular, and just sit there and listen to what people are playing when they're playing spontaneously. And what comes up? You get two or three young men [and] they are going to have some drums and they're going to have what you would call, if you could hear the words, *the Blues.* I can remember just as clear as day, sitting in one of those little villages, up at night, and what they were singin' about had to do with tribulations and all of that.

Dr. Essie Harris
Riverdale, Illinois Public School District 133, Superintendent

From the time I was very, very young, I remember some of the names of some of the great Blues artist of the early '50s. Although I have not followed the Blues as an adult, I still have those memories of the way Blues was introduced to me, and I'm sure to most of the kids in the community. It was through the passage of information down from our parents.

What I have realized as an adult, however, is the last time I went to a Blues fest I was shocked to see the few number of African Americans who were in that group. I was very, very shocked simply because I thought that the Blues might have been something unique to Black people . . . only to find out that the music is appreciated by other ethnic groups, as well.

Dr. Ronald Myer
Baptist Preacher, Jazz Musician & Medical Doctor

Now, remember that the music that the African American's experienced in America came out in a form whether we call it Blues, Gospel, or Jazz that expressed a basic human soul expression. The first inflection of this experience came, in terms of White folks, on the plantations. It began to have a sociological impact in the segregated South as the slave gained freedom and began to move off the plantation.

1.) Wherever the music was played it had a social impact on those who were hearing it from the African Americans who began to express it.

2.) It had an economical impact because it was being recorded as it was being expressed in different settings.

Dr. Frances Carroll
Board of Trustees, University of Illinois

When I was a kid I couldn't stand the Blues because I didn't know what it meant. As I matured, I realized that the words of the Blues really typified what African American people were all about. The Blues seems to be the only medium in which the words and the music capture everything that we do as a people from our living, our working, our loving, and our educational experience—there's a song that typifies all that. So I think it's extremely important that our young people know where the Blues came from.

The socialization portion of the Blues ties us into our history. It ties us into each other, and it helps the elitist and the poorest to understand that we experience the same trials of life. And then for the history, it goes all the way back to the beginning of time, whether or not we go back to the beginning of African Americans in America in the slave time, it illustrates the progress of the African American.

Then the Blues shows where the Black man respects the Black woman because it tells how he loves her; it tells how beautiful her body is; it tells about her cunningness. To me it teaches respect. And no matter how painful relationships are that the Blues talks about, it's like talking about a people rather than an individual, and I think that's why it's become so significant with our people. It's an expression that we have not found in any other music. That's why it'll never die.

Dr. Aldon Morris
Professor of Sociology at Northwestern University
Author of <u>Origins of the Civil Rights Movements</u>

Music is one of the most basic and oldest forms of cultural expressions produced by human beings. It is impossible to conceive of human groups who lack music. This is true because music plays so many functional roles for humanity. Music is utilized as a vast tool of communication for countless purposes. Through it people convey feelings of love, hate, hostility, joy, and pain. Music can be used to justify human oppression and it can serve as the soul of human liberation movements. It can inspire patriotism and it can encourage social criticism.

Music has been very central to the Black experience. The American Black experience has been characterized by suffering and triumph. Black music has been central to these twin pillars of Black existence. Black music has captured the pain of slavery, oppression, exploitation, Jim Crow, and the lynch rope. It has informed the world of the degree to which some human beings will oppress others based on matters as insignificant as skin color. Yet, that same Black music has captured the soul and vision of a people who thirsted to be free and paid the ultimate price for that freedom countless times.

Black music has provided the chain of solidarity for Black people as they marched off to battle in their quest for freedom. When the battle looked bleak, Black music encouraged and conjured up a spirit that could not be defeated. And when triumph emerged, Black music reminded everyone that the Black experience was really a universal experience because we all suffer and triumph, but do so differently.

Dr. George Smith
Psychologist, WVON Radio Talk Show Host

I think it's so important [historically] just like in the Jewish Holocaust. They will not let you forget. Every generation is expected to know about where they've been in order to determine where they're going. The Blues tells our story. It goes way, way back. The slaves used to sit out there and chant words of freedom, direction.

It talks about where we're going. It talks about the plight of a people, where they've been, and where they want to go. It talks about pain. It talks about happiness. It talks about joy, sadness, love, life. It's just the essence of who we are and this is our music.

It belongs to us and it's so good to be able to come back and reclaim it because what has happened is it has been commercialized and we've been somewhat removed from it, and what happens is that we're bringing it back home. It says where we've been is important. Where we're going is important and the people who made up the past are important, and we should never forget where we've been because it will help us determine where we're going. Blues, for us, is not just a music it's a way of life. Historically, it tells a story and we can never stop telling the story. And our young people need to know the story. They need to understand and feel it the way we feel. And the only way they can be able to do that is we have to constantly help remind them.

Dr. Bertrand J. Brown
Education Consultant, New York City Public Schools

Historically, the Blues, as far as our people are concerned, has been an import part of our culture for eons. In point and fact, the Blues is now intercultural and intergroup on this country as well as in other parts of the world. It's impact, universal.

The Blues has always had an outstanding impact on this country's social life. It has colored its music and has become a major form. For Black folks, the Blues has provided a vehicle through which our culture and folklore could be perpetuated from generation to generation. The Blues, as Ralph Ellison so eloquently noted, "is an autobiographical chronicle of personal catastrophe expressed lyrically." It has allowed us an avenue through which we could share our problems and complaints. [We could] share our fears and joys and, yes, even just vent and celebrate! It has also provided other cognitive opportunities for our children. For example, the Blues can be used to teach our kids Math, Reading and creative writing skills, and of course, musical skills. The Blues then becomes an excellent empowering tool for our children and can help our youngsters develop a sense of fate, control, and self-efficacy.

Dr. Charles Mingo
Chicago Public School Administrator

The Blues is really the history of a people. It's not a written history. It's all history in song. The Blues tends to document what was important in the lives of the people. The origins go all the way back to the slave songs in the fields. If you listen to them, they are closely aligned to the old Negro Spirituals, and it talks about the burdens they had.

It's important that young people are exposed to the Blues because it's a part of our history as Black people. We have not just depended on written history [because] much of our history is oral.

Dr. Frank Adams, Sr.
Director of the Alabama Jazz Hall of Fame, Birmingham

Frank Adams played clarinet and alto saxophone for Hilton Jefferson and Johnny Hodges in Duke Ellington's band from 1948-1952. He is featured on the tune entitled *Hawk Talks*.

First of all, the Blues represents a basic human form in its twelve measure structure and simple harmonies. It's easily understood, and it is the basis of a language, a language created here in the Americas. It is a true art form which has no relationship to any other culture but to the Black American culture. It is a fundamental truth that certain things are inherited culturally, and certain things that are inherited culturally speak to life itself.

You also must take into consideration that Black Americans were enslaved for three hundred-fifty years, and we have only been free, if you can say that we are free, and we've only been out of slavery for one hundred fifty-two years. So that's a remarkable thing. We need to keep in touch with our ancestral past. We need to cherish the contributions we have made. In fact, we cannot avoid "not" coming from our past and appreciating it because a person who does not know their past has no concept of the future.

Dr. Jimmy Tillman
Chicago Public School Administrator

First, I believe that in order for us to understand the music we must understand the people who created the music. The Blues is an art form that was developed first in Africa. The Blues was music sang by people regardless of what region they were from. It wasn't called the Blues at that time, it was just the music that they sang.

When those people were captured and put into slavery the sound that was to become known as *the Blues* was developed at that particular time . . . [it] was not actually singing, but it was actually crying. That *blue note,* the flat 7th, the flat 5, those notes that you hear now were the cries of mothers, sisters, and women cryin' either for their husbands, or their sons who were being enslaved. So that particular sound, that wail that brought that pretty harmonious music that we had prior to that time we all call a minor 3rd, or the flatted 7th, or the flatted 5. Those notes came into this musical sound that we brought with us over on that [slave] ship. That sound permeated though the unborn child who was in those African women brought over on those ships. That particular sound became part of our entire being because we were born with it.

Dr. Larry Spruill
Educator in Atlanta, Georgia

The Blues is one of America's most critical folk musics because of how people feel about themselves from a secular point of view. We know about the Spirituals and the Gospels, but the Blues does the same thing for the souls of Black folks. It allows us to express how we feel about what's goin' on in our lives, and when we left the Mississippi Delta, and the Georgia corn fields, and the North Carolina tobacco fields, or wherever we came from in the Southern region. We went northward and it became R&B to some degree.

The Blues, the Blues, the Blues are just an expression of how we feel about living in America. The kids need to hear the Blues because they need to understand much of what they are hearing today comes out of the Blues tradition. It comes out of that tradition where people feel free to say what they need to say about their existence and how they're getting along in this land called America. I have a particular thing about the Blues because I think that kids really, really will love it once they are introduced to it.

We need Blues in our curriculum not only in Afro-American Studies, but the Blues is for White kids, Chinese kids, all kinds of kids need to understand the Blues. I believe that it is an important piece of cultural literacy that kids know what the Blues are. All kids need to know what the Blues are because it's a part of being a literate individual in America and the world today.

Dr. Grace Dawson
DePaul University School Achievement Structure
& Retired Chicago Public School Administrator

I believe that the Blues represents the time line of the Negro people, now African Americans. The things that happened during slavery to Africans formulated the basis for the beautiful tribute that the music called the Blues expresses. The feelings, emotions and dreams of an enslaved people are portrayed in the Blues.

Since the beginning of the music called Blues, Black Americans could relate to all of the expressions that the artists put into their songs and rhythms. Our children can remember their history through the study of the Blues.

No matter how much any other race tries to interpret the Negroes' Blues it is impossible! The experience has to be lived. The experience has to be real. The experience has to be embedded into the people that our Blues represents. I personally believe that the Blues has taken its place in musical history and will always be a part of America and American history. For me, the Blues is the most important form of music expression that I know.

Dr. Doreen E. Barrett
Instructional Designer, Accenture

When we talk about our roots, we need to have young people understand more of our history than our history began with slavery. We are an aesthetic people with our music. We use our music to tell a story. We can use music as a tool for education, and the Blues tells a story with a musical background to it. I think the Blues always gives you examples of something you can relate to.

Herb Kent
Chicago Radio Personality & Broadcast Hall of Fame Member

To me, it is just really good to listen to. I think that those three chords are found in all kinds of music that you hear today. You'd be surprised that a lot of Motown Records [such as] My Girl is a Blues progression. You know? And on, and on, and on. It's just basic and you can go on and build from there.

I don't want to say the Blues is easy to play because it's deceptive. It takes a lot of artistry to perform those Blues. I like the sound. I like the feel that I get when I hear the Blues. There's just something about it which is just so basic. And if you don't like the Blues you've got a hole in your soul.

The Blues means tradition to me. It really takes you back to the roots from the spirituals of which I'm sure the Blues came from. It means a very Black thing to me. It's my our heritage. It's just my heritage.

Charles Hudson
Chicago Public School Administrator

When I was down at Morehouse College [an under graduate] they called me "Charlie Gator," and at that point in time I became the Bluesman at WAUC [The Voice of Atlanta University Center] in Atlanta, Georgia. I was the first Bluesman on the air [there]. It was 1969, my junior year. We also had Roger Bell and Theordrick Harrell. They called us *the Chicago Three*. I played the Blues, Theordrick played Jazz, and Roger played psychedelic music.

When I was doing the Blues in Atlanta, I'd come on the air with Nat King Cole and I'd talk about a little boy that Santa Claus forgot. They didn't have that many Watts, and the girls over at Spelman College and Morris Brown College would say, "Gator, you were great." The Blues is universal. On an ordinary day, we're gonna die, but the Blues will take care of all of it because when you're down and out the Blues is the only place to go.

At that time, the Blues was all we had. I mean [during] the Civil Rights March people were marching and were enthusiastic about being involved in something that they knew they could change by being out there, being a number. Numbers change things. We had the Blues all the time. That's all we had. We had Jazz all the time. It was a little more sophisticated. Even Nat "King" Cole sang [the Blues], "Mona Lisa, Mona Lisa." He loved that woman, but he couldn't get next to her.

"Baby" Ray Horace
Retired Administrator, Chicago Public School

It is extremely important that we preserve the Blues because it's the last form of music that totally belongs to us. They took R&B and made it Rock & Roll. They have taken every facade of our art form and our culture. There's a book called Stolen Legacy where everything we've ever had was stolen.

So we've got to preserve this last bastion of our historicity and our tradition, but beyond that the Blues is an extension of lamentations in the Bible. The original Black Hebrews wrote lamentations, and the Blues that they recorded in our Bible are the same Blues that we have in the Southland and the same Blues we have today.

Those were Black people who wrote and it was very codified and not only were they crying in their own tears, but they were sending secret coded messages to each other the same way that the secret coded messages were done with the art of quilt making. So there are many things in the history of the Blues that we need to keep to ourselves. It's the story of a struggle of a people and it's a beautiful story, and it is something that we must reserve for ourselves and our progeny. Remember, we are still the same people of the Bible from lamentations to the present.

Mahmoud El-Kati
Professor of History at Macalester College, St. Paul, Minnesota
Father of Stokely from the R&B group Mint Conditions

The Blues is a central part of Black life because it says a lot about Blacks through time and space. It's a powerful force in our lives, and it permeates nearly every aspect of our culture. The Blues is the essence of Black life, and it represents a compelling and complex expression of Black folks' humanity. It has been said that the Blues are our "secular" Spirituals. It speaks from the wellsprings of our spirituality in the tradition that the great Negro Spirituals do.

The Blues is a statement and source about our existence. It touches on improvisation and majesty. It shapes other idioms like Jazz, and modern expressions in art including dance. The poets of the '60s such as Nikki Giovanni, Amiri Baraka, and the likes thereof credit the Blues with inspiring their particular genre of poetry.

The Blues has even helped shape the language of writers such as James Baldwin and Langston Hughes. Below is an excerpt of *Weary Blues* by Langston Hughes (1926) as quoted by El-Kati.

> *Droning a drowsy syncopated tune,*
> *Rocking back and forth to a mellow croon,*
>
> *I heard the Negro play.*
> *Down on Lenox Avenue the other night*
>
> *By the pale dull pallor of an old gas light*
>   *He did a lazy sway. He did a lazy sway.*
> *To the tune of those Weary Blues.*

Ernest Dailey
Director of Education and Development,
Hollywood Entertainment Museum

The Blues is important from a historical perspective because it provides insight into a musical and lyrical art form that centers on human experience and a series of events. These events evoke emotions that are happy and sad, funny and serious. The events quite often represent actual historical occurrences that portray the trials, tribulations, and victories of people in the under-served communities of America.

Sociologically, Blues serves as a connection to the ancestry of African Americans linking them to the Motherland, where this art form began. The instruments used to enhance the lyrical value of the Blues have their roots in Africa. Although the Blues is categorized as an art form, we communicators of the Blues all know that the Blues is really a feeling.

Vanessa Bush-Ford
BET (Black Entertainment Television) Weekend Magazine

It comes out of all of the whole musical inheritance we've gotten from slavery. People started singing about their miseries, their lives, the hopes, the dreams, and aspirations they would have. A lot of it branched off into Gospel, and I think the Blues is very much alive in America.

Okoro Harold Johnson
Director, Playwright and Co-Founder of the ETA Creative Arts Foundation

The Blues, to the best of my knowledge, is a musical expression of the pain, the hurt, the horror, and the joy of a people, Black people, living in an oppressed society. The joy is a way of dealing with the pain. This expression was the spontaneous reaction of sensitive and creative individuals.

Theresa Barker
Retired Chicago Public School Special Education Teacher

The Blues is a feeling of soul. It's like an old time religion. Blues to me is a releasing of an inner person and inner feeling that you can put in songs and words. When I listen to it I get a feeling of inner happiness. Listening to the Blues release tension and pressures. It makes you feel free. I can listen to the blues when I feel depressed and it can make me feel good. I don't see the Blues as being stressful or sinful. The words are understandable. It's a connection to other people. You can feel how other people feel.

Victor Woods
Co-author of A Breed Apart

The Blues to me is an expression of people's feelings and thoughts. Having been through some of the trials and tribulations in my life, I listen to the Blues, and one of my favorite people is B.B. King. Often, I think of him and some of his music. One of my favorites from him is, obviously, *the Thrill is Gone*. That has given me some perspective when I've been in relationships.

I think that the Blues to Black people, from a cultural perspective, was a way to express ourselves. From my understanding, the Blues was birthed out of people's sorrows and frustrations. And Black folk, we make beautiful music out of our problems. You can go all the way back to slavery when we were singin' and chopping cotton—a lot of that was singing the Blues . . . coming up with some kind of musical expression that came out of the madness of the situation that we're in. Certain things have been lost today in music, and in our culture. Even though Rap is an expression of the times and how people think, Rap is more of an indictment of a situation making accusations, or stating facts. I think we've lost something in our culture . . . and that's one of the reasons our young people are disconnected because our culture has been ripped from us.

Des Doran
International Development Specialist, Ottawa, Canada

Writing from here in Canada, I see the Blues from the perspective of the Black Diaspora. It is important to remember that many of the Blues artists of the past played not only in Chicago and St. Louis, but also shared their insights into the human soul with audiences in Toronto and Montreal, etc. Today the Blues is everywhere in Canada, from St. Johns in the East to Vancouver in the West.

Bluesmen

Olu Dara
Musician and father of the Rapper Naz

The Blues is really the root of all the music. Period! Everything runs off the Mississippi River; the whole world is biting off the Blues. There are unlimited varieties of the Blues rhythmically, melodically. It's the only music that I know that has unlimited nuances, varieties, rhythms, and melodies.

The Blues is not just indigenous to Black Americans, it's indigenous to the world. When I say *the world* I mean Africa. That's where all the unlimited types of Blues comes from. So I incorporate that in my band so I can go further in root to the Blues.

Fruteland Jackson

It's a legacy. It's our wealth. It's equity. It's what we have. It's all those old records and the work that was put into it, and what we have on this earth that's worth something the moment it's here. It's like a song that's thirty years old, it's still here and it still has the ability to create revenue and royalty. It's part of our rich history. It's our treasure chest. It's where we keep our wealth and our things. So that's why it's important to preserve it and not let it be diluted. If we don't mind newer or contemporary styles, then newer and contemporary styles shouldn't mind us.

Ronnie Baker Brooks

I think the Blues is important because it's the history and the base of American music; music is important to everyone. I think *the Blues is a healer* as John Lee Hooker would say. Whenever a person can relate to something you're singing about it 's like therapy. And they know they're not alone in what they're goin' through—good or bad. I think it's important because of those reasons.

And on the musician side, it's important because it's the basis of all music. You can imply Blues into all styles because Blues is a feeling and a spirit. It's the truth.

Chip Ratliff

Back when I was just a teenager, I met this teacher. Now I'd heard about this teacher all of my life, and he visited the homes in my family quite often, especially on Saturday nights. It seemed as though any party that we had never really got started until he came around. The "teacher" was older and seemed to have been around since the dawn of time, and had a really powerful way of touching peoples' emotions in every way imaginable.

When I finally, begrudgingly, sat down and listened to what the teacher had to tell me, my life was changed. The teacher taught me how to play, what to play, when to play, and when not to play. He taught me what to say and how to say it. It's about how much you can feel it. I was even taught how to dress. He also taught me that one single note, played the right way, can say and mean more than a string of notes played in rapid succession. The teacher is the Blues.

Michael Hill

For me, the Blues is the foundation for African American culture and, therefore, the foundation of a whole lot of American culture. Some people have a narrow concept of the Blues, but for me it's [as] if I'm reading poetry or literature, or if I'm reading James Baldwin or Toni Morrison, or if I see an August Wilson play the Blues is right up in there; the stories my mother and father told me about growin' up in the South.

So for me, the Blues is a whole beautiful and rich fabric to draw from, and it's been salvation for our people here because it's come out of our deepest pain.

The Chicago Harp Monster

The Blues is very important from a cultural standpoint for the fact that it is a music form created by slaves and former slaves. It told of the pain, misery, and sorrow of the people who made it. It also spoke of joy, and of hope. The Blues chronicled life and how the slaves and former slaves saw life. It paints a picture of life, back in a simpler time, in a more physically demanding era. It was, and is, a simple music form, in structure, yet, powerful at the same time.

The most important aspect of the Blues, in my opinion, is that from this very simple music, created by largely an illiterate people, is that it has survived and endured to tell its stories and express its joy. It has survived and matured. It has had offspring and has branched out. The evidence, my friend, is in Rhythm & Blues, Rock & Roll, Jazz, Gospel, and Soul music.

Charlie Love

Why is it important that young Blacks learn about and play the Blues? A reason is that the Blues involves an evolution that jump-started a nation. Because of it you have Jazz, Rap, and Pop music. The Blues is a receipt that we as African Americans can claim as ours. It's part of our history. The Blues is important because Black people are not exposed to the Blues on a national level. We must incorporate our minds and keep the Blues alive by listening and expressing it musically.

The Blues is a universal spiritual awakening to life's everyday situations. Why is the Blues recognized by the President of the United States, the Governors and Mayors? Do you really want to know? Well, I am not going to tell you, but I will urge you to visit a Blues club and experience the reason why.

Larry McCray

The Blues deserves preservation as much so as any dying species of endangered animal(s) or anything that's precious to anyone in this world that deserves to be protected and passed to the new generation. Just like you couldn't see what the world would be like without deer, bears, and tigers, what would the world be like without the Blues?

For some people it regulates their normality in life. Sometimes the only thing that can soothe the savage beast is the right music for the right occasion. For me, most occasions happen to be the Blues.

Melvin Smith

Black children in America need to realize and make contact with their heritage [of] which is what's rightfully theirs because it's a music that's delivering a message of history. Things that have happened in the past that they'll always be able to come back and relate it to the future and present. Our music is something that other people are trying to steal away and claim it as theirs, and our children need to develop it and remember that it's always something from their soul, and their hearts, and their ancestors.

Gregg Parker

Well, the Blues is our culture, and it's really the only thing that we can claim. Nowadays, it seems harder for us to do either as performers, archivists, and journalists because we don't really own any of it.

The significance of the Chicago Blues Museum is that it takes a stand on representing everybody involved in the Blues, not an individual, and everybody that derives from the Blues.

David "Biscuit" Miller

The Blues means to me being free to speak out my feelings about life—the good and the bad times. Even young people have Blues today. I don't care if it's Rock & Roll, Country, R&B, or Soul it's all related to the root of the Blues. The feeling of being free to express yourself.

Stan Skibby

I believe the Blues is the root of all-American music. It is the basics of all-American music. It's our first music experience as Black folks this country.

Fernando Jones

The Blues is a good thing. It's the whole process of Black folks in America creating something out of nothing.

Mervyn "Harmonica" Hinds

The Blues is life. It's a feeling of life when you are up or when you are down. The musical form has it's origins in Africa. Very often the Blues is equated with sadness because of the feeling it evokes. People tend to remember sadness quicker rather than gladness. They think of negativity quicker rather than positivity. Hence, the reason why the Blues is associated with the gloomy side of things rather than the bright side.

<u>It's time for the show to start so find the missing Bluesman</u>

```
L L N I V L E M N O I R R G W
P F R U T E L A N D O I I Y P
V O I P R A H K M N I X K X H
T P I H C H X O N A T S E S G
W A T I U C S I B N G V U E M
L F D N K I E Y R R A L K D E
D A I D Y M S N E E O Y U P J
B T E S M H Q G F F T U M T X
D E S J X Q G J J G V I E D N
T L M B P Q B A S J U F C P K
```

**BISCUIT • CHIP • FERNANDO • FRUTELAND • GREGG • HARP • HINDS
LARRY • MELVIN • MICHAEL • OLU • RONNIE • STAN**

FIVE
A Blueswoman's Perspective

From inception Black women have been a big part of the Blues experience. She gave the Blues life and a reason to live. In the 1920s and '30s, women such as Gertrude "Ma" Rainey, Ida Cox, Bessie Smith, and Mamie Smith were called Vaudeville Blues singers. Though their voices, in some cases, were as gritty as the men's, their musical accompaniments were much smoother. Back then, a woman singing the Blues was considered to be low-class.

Sally Placksin, author of <u>American Women in Jazz: 1900 to the Present</u> wrote: "From Africa Black men and women brought a birthright and blood right of music—a heritage of improvisation, rhythm, call-and-response, antiphony, and a musical passion that would be retained in America."

Nikki Ayanna Stewart, Ph.D. candidate from the University of Maryland, said, "Can you imagine the Blues without Ma Rainey? Bessie Smith? Can you imagine the Blues without the voices of Black women? Farah Jasmine Griffin, author of the book '*In Search of Billie Holiday: If You Can't Be Free, Be a Mystery*' argues that the Black female voice is the voice of America.

Fernando Jones

"From Marian Anderson, to Mahalia Jackson, to Aretha Franklin, the Black female voice represents the very soul of America. Since Black women are subjected to brutal oppression they have always played important roles in transforming this country into a better nation. Their voices simultaneously communicate the depths of a nation's pain, and the heights of its joy.

"From a historical perspective, it has always been easier to study the lives of middle class Black women than working class Black women because middle class women tend to leave personal papers when they pass on. This means that a lot of our ideas about Black women in the past have only come from the records of middle class highly educated Black women. However, during the last ten years, Black feminist scholars like Bell Hooks, Hazel Carby, and Angela Davis have begun to systematically study the lives and lyrics of Blues women like Ma Rainey and Bessie Smith. Since Rainey and Smith wrote many of their own songs, their songs are historical documents that can give insight into the lives of working class Black women—women who don't necessarily leave letters, diaries, and full-length autobiographies.

"As a Chicago native, I grew up surrounded by the Blues. And I like knowing that the voices of Blues women keep singing to me as a researcher on Black women, promising once again to transform our understanding of America."

Here are some Blueswomen who have carried the torch and tradition. There is fire, passion, truth, peace, and spirituality in each and every one of these women in this section. To read their stories will enhance your musicological being. Read and relax.

KoKo Taylor
"I think all of the young people, boys and girls, rich, poor, Black or White, especially the Blacks, should appreciate the Blues because the Blues is a reminder of slavery. That's where the Blues all started from, and came from. And a lot of the young Blacks that were born and raised in Chicago, Detroit, and other big cities—a lot of them think we're crazy for playing the Blues, but the Blues is our culture, they don't know that Blues belongs to Blacks because that's where it came from."

•On the next page is a song I wrote in hopes of Ms. KoKo recording someday.

58

Danger Sign
by Fernando Jones 12/11/92
*Inspired by KoKo Taylor.
©1992
Bluefunkjazroll Music, BMI

I came from the South With the Blues on my knee.
Sang 'em from a baby (That's why) I'm the Queen.

When I groove / I cruise in Cadillacs.
And when I move / you better stand back.
        Cuz I'm KoKo Taylor / a danger sign.
        I cut like a razor (and) I'll blow yo' mind.

I'm KoKo Taylor / That's my name.
I rock uh room of Blues like uh hurricane.

If you gamble / gamble on me.
If you love me / set me free.

I'm a lady. I'm a man's desire.
I'm 10 miles of fire wrapped in barbwire.
        I'm KoKo Taylor / a danger sign.
        I cut like a razor (and) I'll blow yo' mind.

I'm KoKo Taylor / That's my name.
I rock uh room of Blues like uh hurricane.

I got money, and I got time.
Men like me because I'm so fine.

There ain't nothin' / That I can't do.
I got a gold credit card and a diamond one, too.
        I'm KoKo Taylor / a danger sign.
        I cut like a razor (and) I'll blow yo' mind.

Theresa Needham

In 1968, my brother, Foree, took me to Theresa's Lounge. I was four. It was located in the basement of an apartment building at 4801 S. Indiana Ave. T's was operated solely by a little woman from Mississippi named Theresa Needham. We all affectionately called her "T." Fans and musicians came to T's from all over the world. This club was so special because most of the nightclubs with live Black entertainment in Chicago back then were owned and operated by White men.

In its heyday, her club was the most famous Blues joint in the world. My brothers, Foree, Greg, and Marvin, my cousins, Robert Earl, Flicker, and W.C., and my brother-in-law, Herman, were regulars at T's. On weekends, the "corner" was accented with fancy cars and all kinds of cool *hep-cats* sharply dressed. The ladies were so fine and they made me wish I were grown. Conversations always flowed and everybody was famous for one reason or another—on the corner.

Though classified as *a hole in the wall,* affectionately, local musicians and singers presented themselves on Theresa's tiny stage as if they were performing at Carnegie Hall. Foree said, "Theresa's was home for me. I got a lot of good gigs from singing down there. I got my first big gig at the Marriot O'Hare Hotel when a man named Rob from the Elks in Robbins, Illinois saw me at Theresa's." Her club was more than a *club* it was a social and cultural center.

Theresa said, "I opened a tavern at 4801 S. Indiana in 1948. I had White, Colored, and everybody in my club. They'd even come from out of town. I stayed there [for] thirty-five years. People used to go to church on Sunday morning before tavern time and when they got out they'd make it down to the basement. I used to cook pig-ears and pig-feet. When I first opened up, I used to let the teenagers in and I'd make them sit in the corner booths. I enjoyed it. Yeah, sometimes I lay down and cry when I think about those days. If they [patrons] got too high or couldn't leave, I'd let them sit over in the booth until they sobered up.

"I remember the police picked up a bunch [of teenagers] for curfew. That was when the police station was on 48th & State. And they came and got me and said, 'We got some of your customers over here. You better come get 'em out!' I said, 'What the hell did you bother them for in the first place?' I went over there and they turned them loose."

On one of the Blue Monday Blues shows Barry Dolins brought his adult education class out to Theresa's Lounge. Barry said, "Junior Wells was there and he opened his attaché case and explained all of the different harmonicas. Those were fond memories."

"If you wouldn't of kicked the door down, you wouldn't of caught me in the bed with your w-i-i-i-fe," said Muddy Waters, Jr. as he kicked off a tune in the winter of 1985 at the New Theresa's Lounge. He said, "I got started in 1955. My first gig was with Levi at Theresa's Lounge."

Eddie Butler reflected on his first night at T's: "It sounded like it was a jukebox playing down there at first, and then I walked into the place. I was only about nineteen, and the first person I met was Junior Wells. I told him that I wanted to play with them. It was just like a dream come true. I got applause and captivated the audience."

Gerri Oliver

FJ: How long has Gerri's Palm Tavern been in existence?

GO: It was opened in 1933 by James Knight, our first Mayor of Bronzeville. In 1956, I bought it from Mr. Knight and the doors have managed to stay open since that time. However, that was the last of the glory days of South Park and Regal Theater. This was their home away from home for the all stars. They were not stars or rich yet, and they looked forward to me fixing them some home cooked meals because they were used to eating sandwiches on the road. I would put them up in some cases until draw day on Monday. They came into town on Thursdays and played on Friday, Saturday, and Sunday.

FJ: How was it being among the few female club owners in Chicago at that time?

GO: We weren't really so rare. It was just that we were in one place for so long. I'm still at 446-48 East 47 Street.

FJ: Who were some of the artists that hung out at the club?

GO: Johnny Hodges, Count Basie, Quincy Jones, the Flamingos, the Vibrations, Louis Jordan, Ruth Brown, James Brown, Ray Charles, LaVern Baker, Chuck Willis, David Newman, Big Joe Turner, T-Bone Walker, Champion Jack Dupree, Dionne Warwick, Dee Clark, Eugene Church, Eddie "Lock Jaw" Bates, Sonny Boy Williamson, Gene Chandler, Big Maybelle, Jerry Butler, Curtis Mayfield, Percy Mayfield, the Coasters, Dinah Washington, the Drifters, Butter Beans & Suzie, Scottie Piper (the Mayor of 47th Street). Just to think I knew all of those people when they were not famous. Nobody! You have to realize that they basically were all on the same circuit doing theaters in different towns and they'd stop here. This was their home away from home.

FJ: How did the artists dress back then?

GO: Everybody was sharp! Nobody would be caught out there with tennis shoes on. Are you kidding?

FJ: Paint a picture of how 47th Street used to be.

GO: It was Broadway for Black people and Black entrepreneurs. It was the top of the line like the Mecca.

FJ: How were the crowds channeled from the Sutherland Hotel to the Regal and back to your place?

GO: We used to exchange patronage. The artists would more or less relax here.

FJ: When was the 'great fall' of 47th Street?

GO: Around 1968 when they had James Brown at the Regal, the crowd tore the theater up then they closed it down after that. Then they had gang wars later on that drove many of the Jewish merchants away, and that was it.

Sydney Ellis

While thumbing through Living Blues Magazine, I noticed an ad for Sydney's CD and emailed her. She graciously granted me an interview. Sydney lives in Germany, but was born in Red Jacket, West Virginia. When asked about the global attraction to the Blues she replied: "I don't think it is 'Blues' that is attractive globally, but instead there has always been a market worldwide for quality artists, entertainers, musicians, and singers whether it's Americans traveling the world, or artists from all over the world performing and bringing their particular art to the United States. This has been true through out time. As far as 'Blues' goes, I wouldn't think that anybody who wants to make a lot of money would wake up and say, 'I've got it. I know how to make a lot of money. I'll become a Blues Musician.' Music, and particularly Blues, draws singers and musicians to it because it touches something in their heart and soul, and it becomes an obsession. Something they cannot *not* do. I think music and the arts have its own way of creating that obsession in people. That's why they do it.

"To me, Blues is not an it. It is not something I do. It's just part of everyday life. There is no way to separate 'it' from me. At the same time I know and have heard a lot of Americans (non Afro-Americans) that can really play or sing Blues, and this goes to show that when one generalizes, one also has to acknowledge exceptions. The reason for those exceptions is that above anything else Blues is a feeling. It's not the form of a song. It's not the chord progressions, or the instrumentation. It is the feeling! This is why when I interview a sideman about playing for me I ask him or her what kind of music they play. If they say, 'All kinds, Bebop, Rock & Roll, Jazz, Soul, R&B, [or] whatever,' if they don't answer, 'Just Blues,' then I will hesitate in hiring them because the best Blues musicians I have heard or know don't play any other kind of music. Not because they can't, it's just they don't want to. It's the obsession. Artists who do not play anything else are the ones who have the obsession. Those are the ones I want to play with. The others, they haven't found their obsession yet, and it's not necessarily sincere or honest."

Shirley King

When asked about the discrimination Blueswomen face Shirley said, "It's not that I'm asking for more respect for Blueswomen over Bluesmen, but what I'm seeing in the music world is that there are very few Blueswomen out here headlining and being able to control a show like a Bluesman. Being a bandleader myself, and a female, I encounter the same problems. I might go somewhere and people will accept me and open up doors and let me in because I'm B.B. King's daughter, not because it's Shirley King. You find yourself having to fight off the people you work for because if you say no [to a job], you might not work no more.

"I just feel like women singers don't get the respect even if you are a band leader they kind of want to go to your band leader and talk to him because it's a man thing. You know? A lot of times the women don't get a chance to work that much and the audiences are saying, "We want to see more women performers. We like women performers better blah, blah, blah," but it's not helping us because a lot of us don't work that much.

"I feel [that] if the woman get together, bond together, and unite to do Blues and everything . . . knowing that people want to see them, they can kind of demand more. Maybe they don't know that they are as important to Blues music as they are. From what I'm hearing, people want to see more women. Now, when that reaches the promoters and club owner, maybe we'll gain a little respect.

Katherine Davis

Katherine started singing in the church choir as a child while growing up in Chicago's Cabrini Green Housing Project. Later, her interests turned to the Opera. She learned to sing in French, German, and Italian. However, the desire to sing in Blues clubs took precedence over singing in Opera houses.

Katherine said, "Take all of the people who are going to church and put them in a the clubs. And place all of the Blues people in the church. Then there would be a big difference because being a Blues artist is just like being a preacher to the lay people. As a child, I hadn't been exposed to the Blues to the point where I was proud of it. My parents had parties and they would play Blues, but if I tried to sing it, it was a no, no." In 1977, Ms. Davis was featured as Gertrude "Ma" Rainey and Bessie Smith in *The House of the Blues.*

Barbara LeShoure

Barbara started singing when she was two years old. In 1967, she went to Israel on a tour that turned out to be a scam in her own words. "It was depressing because the guy that was heading the organization tricked everybody into selling their houses, cars, and everything trying to live a life of what we called 'truth.' And when we got there we found out that we were being 'played on.' After I found out we were being tricked I hitch hiked on up to Tel Aviv, Israel from Demona to get some money from the American Embassy so I could get back home. It was a very ugly experience and scary. [And you] talk about the Blues?"

Barbara is as immaculate on stage as she's outspoken. "This is the way I started out at the Kingston Mines and I got ridiculed for changing clothes for the shows three times a night. The girls scorned me for that. You all can't keep on trying to scorn me because this is the way *you* are supposed to look on stage. I started to get mad and beat them up. They made me mad, but I said there was

Fernando Jones

another way to deal with this. When you hit the stage you have to get the audience. It's a spiritual vibe and you have to lock 'em in and make 'em listen.

"Oh, honey, jealousy is something else, Fernando. Jealousy is a bad demon! They didn't know any better. And no! They are not gonna dog me. I'll quit first, and you know I ain't quitting, so they are not gonna flat out dog me. That's all. If I were going to quit I would have done that a long time ago because I've been misused and abused. And they wonder why I sing the Blues so good. If you don't take your foot off of my neck I can't ever stop singing."

Big Time Sarah
FJ: How did you get started?
BT: I started singing Gospel at the age of five, and from there I got into the Blues, Rock & Roll, and Soul, but I stuck with Blues because it was the only thing that really made me some money.
FJ: How hard is it for women Blues artists to make it?
BT: We got it real hard. You see, male artists think they can just throw us in a corner. But now there are so many women singers out here that all they can do is give us a chance.
FJ: How do you and the other women pull together in these situations?
BT: Doin' our thing and saying stand to the side because we women are gonna take over.
FJ: What would you like to share with the world?
BT: Everybody sings a little different, but when it comes to the Blues and it's done right, it's still called the Blues.

Nellie Travis
The Blues is just like hot sugar, baby, it's good when you melt it down. You know? It's all about the soul, all about the mind, all about what you're feelin' within your heart and your spirit.

I live the Blues everyday. What I see is what I feel. What I feel is what I feel. I guess I said that right. If it doesn't make sense, that's what the Blues is. I've been doin' the Blues for eleven years, [and have] been feelin' that feelin' for about fifteen [years]. It's all about being alive in the Blues.

Don't Mess With My Man
by Fernando Jones 3/15/00
©2000
Bluefunkjazroll Music, BMI

I'll give you the shirt off my back.
And give you the keys to my Cadillac.
> *(Refrain)*
> *But when it comes to love / I'm a hurricane.*
> *When it comes to love / don't mess with my man.*

64

You can talk about me 'til it makes me shamed.
You can lose all of my jewelry in a dice game.
        (Refrain)
You can set my mink coat on fire.
And throw it in the rain if you desire.
        (Refrain)
You can take a $100 out my pocket,
And leave me change to go to the market.
        (Refrain)

Shiri Riley

The Blues means a musical connection to my past and my future. They say you don't know where you're going unless you know where you've been. It's the life stories that I share with my ancestors. I know my great grandmother cried over a lost love. I know her mother did too. And I know they both sang about it, and found comfort in Blues and Gospel music just like I do now. And my daughter will, too.

The first time I sang in public, I was very shy. The audience didn't react until I sang a Blues song. I always felt a lot when I heard Blues songs played, but when I finally worked up enough courage to sing one myself, I heard so much in the spaces of those notes. Some people think the Blues is so simple and easy, but I hear so much in between those spaces, and I see so much color in those notes. I like the way they bend and moan. I love the stories. I love the characters. To me, it is like painting with a whole spectrum of blue shades. I love to paint stories when I sing the Blues.

In Love With A Blues Man
by Fernando Jones 3/93
Recorded by Shiri Riley
©1993
Bluefunkjazroll Music, BMI

Doo doo doo
        Doo doo doo doo doo doo
Doo doo doo
        Doo doo doo doo doo doo
Mama, I'm in love with a Bluesman.
Don't try and understand.
He stays out all night,
And he ain't got a nine to five,
But he treats her nice.
        Mama, I'm in love with a Bluesman . . .
        Mama, I'm in love with a Bluesman . . .
        A Bluesman, a Bluesman.

In 12 bars he seduces me.
In every key unloosens me.
I know he loves me
And you might not approve
Of me and the man of Blues.
          Mama, I'm in love with a Bluesman . . .
          Mama, I'm in love with a Bluesman . . .
          A Bluesman, a Bluesman.

          A lament for me he never plays.
          His love for me is all I crave.
          He's my everything and all I need
          I'm in love, mama, can't you see.
                    Mama, I'm in love with a Bluesman . . .
                    Mama, I'm in love with a Bluesman . . .
                    A Bluesman, a Bluesman.

Smoke filled rooms is all he knows.
He wears his hats ace-deuce and loud color clothes.
He's got a mouth like a sailor.
But he treats me like an angel.
When we're together, I'm all that matters.
          Mama, I'm in love with a Bluesman . . .
          Mama, I'm in love with a Bluesman . . .
          A Bluesman, a Bluesman.

Doo doo doo
          Doo doo doo doo doo doo
Doo doo doo
          Doo doo doo doo doo doo

After visiting Dr. Caleb Dube's "Chicago Blues and Jazz" Freshmen class at DePaul University on Wednesday, September 30, 2003, here in Chicago, Shavonne Moore said this about the Blues: "The Blues is a brand new exciting experience for me. As old as the Blues is, to a young Clevelander like myself, my first experience came as a college student. That experience was one of the best of my life. I have always been told that the Blues was for people who had a broken heart, lost their job, or just had a hard time in life. Singing the Blues puts a smile on my face and lifts up my spirits. To me, the Blues is like a rainbow of different feelings and interpretations.

S I X
A Bluesman's Perspective

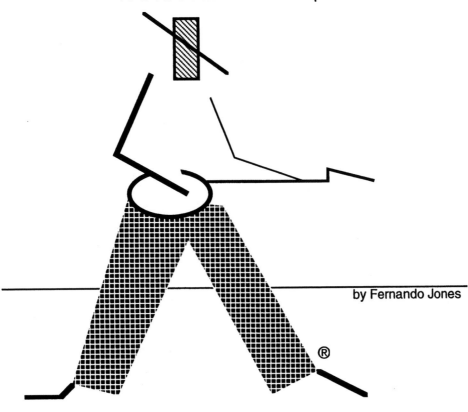

by Fernando Jones

In my shoes I walk the Blues. I walk the Blues in my shoes
Everyone knows who I am except you and my family.
I built the ladder that you climb so easily.
In my shoes I walk the Blues. I walk The Blues in my shoes.

Before we get off into this section, I'd like to share a little bit about myself. When I was about four years old I started playing the guitar and broom, while listening to all types of music. My brother, Greg, had a band called Savage Import, and they practiced at our apartment on 55 East 60th Street. That was my introduction to live music. And like the American Federation of Musicians says, "Live music is the best."

Usually, when they'd finish rehearsing, it would be too late to break the equipment down so they'd leave it until the next day. In addition to the music, they always had pretty girls around. That was enough. Anyway, Greg would say stuff like, "Don't bother this [equipment]. It isn't mine." And like all good little brothers, I didn't listen. I banged on the drums, plucked the keyboard, and strummed the guitars.

The drums belonged to his best friend, Michael Jackson, who lived across the street from us on Wabash. The guitar I practiced on belonged to their band mate, Moscow. That guitar was extremely heavy. Sometimes I'd play until the tips of my fingers were sore. At the same time, I hoped a string wouldn't break because that would have given me away.

Interview with Fred Winston
WLS 890 AM Friday, July 14, 1989

FW:Huey Lewis & the News . . . 6:11AM . . .WLS Chicago, the home of the Blues. Would you not say so Fernando Jones?

FJ: Sure would!

FW:It's my buddy, Fernando, who is one of Chicago's premier guitar players. And when he finishes his current project and gets it published he will be known as, along with one of Chicago's premier guitarists, [a] Chicago Blues historian. Fernando has been working on a project to document the Blues in Chicago. Give me a little background on it for those who don't know.

FJ: First of all, I would like to say thank you, Fred, for having me on this morning. And the name of the project is called "I Was There When The Blues Was Red Hot." Basically, what I'm trying to do with the project is preserve and cultivate the Blues. And give something back to the people like Junior Wells, Sugar Blue, Lefty Dizz, and the 43rd Street Bluesmen who have given me so much. I figure it's the least that I can do.

FW: How come all of these English guys like to sit in with the Chicago Bluesmen? What is the attraction [for them]? I know what it is for me.

FJ: Well, basically, a lot of the guys like Mick Jagger and Eric Clapton . . . when they were growing up they were very big on Chess Records. So, they felt like if they could ever get to America they wanted to come to Chicago because that was the home of Chess Records. You had so many different artists here. Willie Dixon was still living here. You have Sugar Blue still here, Junior Wells is still here, Buddy Guy. That's the attraction. You can come and hit a club and see about five living legends.

FW: Hey, Fernando nice talkin' with you, buddy.

FJ: Thank you for having me. And thank you Chicago.

Downhome Bluesmen

Downhome Blues was played by rural Bluesmen in the 1920s, '30s, and '40s. Their songs were relatively simple to produce and record because many artists accompanied themselves either by playing guitar, harmonica, or piano.

Blind players such as Blind Lemon Jefferson popularized the National Steel and Dobros style guitars. Steel guitars projected sound brighter and louder than conventional acoustic ones. Therefore, this type of guitar was perfect for playing house and rent parties as well as street corner gigs, too. As a child, I saw Blind Arvella Gray play his steel guitar on Saturday afternoons when my mother used to take me shopping with her on 63rd & Halsted. He'd sing for tips in front of the dime store. He had a tin cup dangling from the head of his guitar for tips. Man, he was mean.

Rooted deeply in the tradition of the African American experience, Downhome Bluesman generally constructed songs based on relationships, environment, ego, and superstition.

Relationships: The display of emotional and physical desires, wants, and needs.
Environment: Travel, geography, topography.
Ego: Self-aggrandizement, virility, super human strength, freedom, immortality.
Superstition: Black cats, lucky charms, cat bones, magic numbers, potions, signs, roots, spells, sweeping brooms, jumping eyes, itching hands, ringing ears, etcetera.

L.C. Thurman
Proprietor of the Checkerboard Lounge

The Checkerboard Lounge was opened by Buddy Guy and L.C. Thurman in 1972. L.C. said, "Blues clubs are hard. You can't get rich, but a few have made it. I have fun here. That's why I'm here."

FJ: What was a proud moment for you here?
LC: It was a proud moment for me when Chuck Berry came here and played a whole set. That really surprised me. That was exciting.
FJ: Did he call before he came?
LC: No, he didn't. He just came by surprise, and that's what excited me. Chuck Berry and Keith Richards of the Rolling Stones came by together. They came and played a whole set. And we couldn't get the people to leave out of the club. When the Rolling Stones came, their road manager came up to me and said, "We want to rent the place on a Sunday in July of 1982." I said, 'I'm having a birthday party on that day for a lady named Aretta.' Then he said, "Is the birthday party more important than me renting the club from you?" I said, 'Man I don't know. I have to let you know later. I have to talk to her and see what she'll say about it.' So they looked around and left. They wouldn't let me know who they were. So they came back the next night and told me they wanted to do a video with Muddy Waters and Mick Jack [Jagger]. Then I said, 'Man, you're kiddin' me.' Then he said, "No, I'm serious." Then he showed me his identification. I talked to Mick Jack on the phone. Man, I could hardly believe it. I said, Y'all can have the place. It took me the whole day to set up the equipment. We could fit only so many people in here. We had so many people down here we had to have the police block the street off at 43rd & Vincennes.

Big Bill Collins walked in the club while we were talking (Wednesday, April 19, 1989) and started talking. "The Rolling Stones used to call me," he said, "down at the station. They love the Blues." I used to listen to Big Bill on WNIB late nights in the '80s. He'd say, "I'm Big Bill, down in the basement sittin' on my beat-up, giant, economy size orange crate. I got a feelin' that you don't want to hear the Blues this morning . . . and this goes out to all of my listeners in my bordering states."

> *A smoky night club cutting notes.*
> *Hard to breathe for the music is the smoke.*
> *Night time, night time where can you be?*
> *Create the atmosphere so I can be free.*
> *Night time, night time lend me your ear*
> *For the hole in the wall is calling, calling me near.*

Buddy Guy & Junior Wells

On May 20, 1988, my brother, Foree, and I went to Biddy Mulligan's to see Buddy Guy. He invited us on stage to play a couple of tunes with him. A few months later, on September 17, 1988, Buddy and Junior Wells performed there together. Buddy went on first, while my college friend Ron Robertson, Junior, who I called Godfather, and I were in the dressing room talkin' and laughing loud. All of a sudden the crowd went wild. Buddy was walking through the crowd, as his assistant, James Williams, was trailed him keeping his long orange guitar cord from tangling. When he stepped back on stage, he cranked up his honey-gold colored Guild guitar and unleashed an earth shaking sound through his Marshall amplifier.

After the set, his band went right into the introduction for the Godfather. Usually, when the Godfather would hit the stage Buddy'd leave. But this night, Buddy stayed. I don't remember the tune, but do remember the energy. As a matter of fact, I'm groovin' as I write and think about it. If I'm not mistaken, neither had a record deals at the time. During the Godfather's song he sang:

> *Can I feel it if I wanna feel it? Can I touch it if I wanna touch it?*
> *Big fat woman with the meat shakin' on her bones.*
> *Makes a little skinny [expletive] like me*
> *Wanna come back home and I throw up my hands.*
> *You're just too young to understand.*

After his set, the Godfather left the stage, and Buddy stayed and teased the audience with more medleys of the songs he planned on doing for his next show. He stepped to the microphone and said, "When I come back I'm gonna play (he played a riff that led into *Sunshine of Your Love* by Cream). Y'all thought I forgot? I ain't forgot [expletive]." After that, he went into the Band of Gypsys' song *Who Knows*. The audience went into a frenzy. He ended the medley by excusing his band, and did an imitation of John Lee Hooker singing *Boogie Chillen*. Buddy

70

once told me, "Some might out play me, but no one will out do me. If push comes to shove I've got a trick where I'll throw my guitar down and run across it."

Tom Marker said this to me on April 19, 1989: "I think the albums that they [Junior Wells and Buddy Guy] did on Delmark are among my favorites ever. I just get such a charge out of those. Maybe it's just because that's when I really started listening to Blues records. I like seeing Junior Wells and Buddy Guy, but when they get together it's still real magical for me. It seems like it's just better than anything else you see. Anyone else is no where as special. I'm just crazy about 'em."

Lefty Dizz

Dizz was slim, trim, and always dressed to kill. On stage his partner in crime, *the Baby,* was a beat-up 1968 black Fender Stratocaster. "Don't send for me because if you do, I just might show up. And if I do, it's gonna be a mess I tell ya!" That was Dizz's favorite phrase of phrases. He got part of his name from being left handed; the other half came from playing trumpet and patterning himself after Dizzy Gillespie as a child. He reflects: "Blues was something that we could hear in our home and on our way to school. Back at that time, all of the record stores would be playing Blues with the speakers outside. You'd hear it everyday."

He was the most sophisticated, yet down to earth person you'd ever want to meet. Dizz was witty. No, he was hilarious. And on the South side of Chicago humor in many cases is better protection than a knife or gun.

In 1955, Lefty Dizz started "fooling around with the guitar" when he was stationed in Korea. There, a pilot in the United States Air Force, he learned how to play guitar in eight months. By that time he was playing professionally. "A musician is like a doctor or a lawyer. You practice law, medicine, and you practice music. There is a lost chord out there and nobody has found it yet. So you have to keep on searching for it. Every time I pick up my guitar I learn something new. When I started going to nightclubs I'd hear and see the Blues. That's visual. I'd see artists and say, 'Hell, I can do that.' It wasn't that easy at first because the Blues wasn't written. It is and was felt. When you start to play it, you can tell the difference. I'm not any better than anyone else, but I'm as good as anybody else." By the way, Dizz earned a degree in Economics from Southern

Fernando Jones

Illinois University. By the 1960s, while many of his contemporaries recorded for Chess Records he recorded for king.

When Dizz started playing professionally, he played with country Bluesmen who in his words "would not sing on time, and changed when they felt like it. Once you got the hang of it and learned how to lay back and wait on the vocalist, then you'd have no problem."

Dizz said, "Junior Wells and I took the Blues into Canada. We took our Chicago Blues into Canada. And Canada hasn't been the same since. What I mean is that the only people that would go up there were Sonny Terry and Brownie McGhee, and they worked together for sixty years." Dizz was Junior's guitar player at Expo '67. Dizz's brother, Woody Williams, played drums, Doug Fagan was on sax and Willie Monroe was on bass.

When Lefty Dizz was working with Sonny Thompson the manager of the King Recording Company he met and befriended Jimi Hendrix. "He met me when he was fourteen years old in Seattle, Washington. That was around the time he was learning how to play. When we came to the club they would let him come back stage and talk to me." Dizz played with the likes of Little Esther Phillips, Woody Flemings, Dee Clark, and Ben E. King.

Terry "Tut" Morrissette said, "When you think about Hendrix, you wouldn't think about a Blues player, but that's what he played. He was a Blues *cat* He just had his own concept of how he delivered it." Hendrix played his guitar upside down with the strings reversed. Dizz, however, gave a different description of his left handed style by saying, "I just invert my mind, and step on it."

Top sayings of Lefty Dizz:
30. You're a fourteen karat fool.
29. It's a tough [expletive], but [the] baby's gotta get the milk.
28. We gonna throw down like we live.
27. Once you die, you got it made.
26. And the band played on.
25. You 'bout a dumb [expletive].
24. I'm not the White man's fool 'cause I went to the White man's school.
23. Don't make me get Black.
22. Step into my office.
21. Blood is thicker than mud.
20. There'll be peace in the valley or we'll fight in the alley.
19. I wear the [expletive].
18. All you can do is throw out the line, and watch the cork bob on top.
17. I didn't stutter, there's nothing wrong with my diction.

16. When I grow up I wanna be just like you . . . a big dummy.
15. The more books I buy you, the more pages you tear out.
14. Shut up, dumb boy!
13. I'll throw a firecracker in a Chinese parade.
12. Get away. Get away.
11. I am the baby.
10. I'll throw a brick at a hearse.
 9. I don't cuss 'til after midnight.
 8. Now, where's my money?
 7. Don't do me!
 6. What ever you do don't panic!
 5. I'm not amused.
 4. I'm the *Guitar Wiz,* Lefty Dizz!
 3. I spoke! I have spoken.
 2. I'm not the village idiot.
 1. Don't invite me because if you do I might just show up.
And if I do, it's gonna be a mess I tell ya!

With his hat cocked ace-deuce
Draped in shark skinned suits
Drankin' Grand Dad . . . 100 pounds of rocket juice.
Serious as a brick,
Yet playful as a lamb,
Prolific as Puskin and always a Bluesman.

Woody Williams

It was an unseasonably warm Saturday evening on January 21, 1989, but it was not half as "hot" as the show that Woody Williams put on at the Wrigley Side that night. To kick off the show Lefty Dizz said, "Now I'm about to announce a man who mom and dad brought from the hospital, and I've been calling him brother ever since." Then Woody said, "By being raised in a Blues family, I grew up with the Blues on an everyday basis."

Woody was the drummer for Junior Wells' band in the '60s. He said, "I enjoy the music. Hell, I've been doing it for twenty-five years, now. Hopefully, I can squeeze another ten out of me. I do a lot of Rhythm & Blues, which is nothing but a spin-off of the Blues. Everybody knows that, and everybody who doesn't know should have a pretty good understanding about it anyway. All you have to do is listen to all of the Rock & Roll and Jazz groups. Hell, Blues was originally created here in this land and all of the other people brought their music with them. It was created here through the turmoil and the struggle. The Blues speaks for itself."

FJ: Where is the future of the Blues going? How do you get young Blacks interested?

W W: In order to get people involved, especially young Black people, you have to have air-play. Many of the young White college kids are more aware of the Blues, and they can name you more traditional Blues songs. Some can even tell you what key the songs were originally recorded in.

FJ: What's the reason?

WW: They don't play it on the radio stations. Some of the stations will play a variety of Heavy Metal Rock & Roll, but they'll always give credit to the older Blues Masters.

FJ: Where has this music taken you?

WW: I have traveled the world three or four times in the last twenty-five years. I've been to Japan, Canada, Europe, the West Coast of Kenya, and the Caribbean Islands. Overseas, people appreciate the music a lot more because they don't have the artists over there who have lived the struggle of the Blues. Now, people in Europe and Japan are beginning to "play" the old traditional Blues. And they're playin' it. They love the Blues, and I love it!

Chicago Beau

"My father bought a brand new car in 1959, and before we got it off the lot I asked him if I could turn the radio on. I flipped the radio on and there was a song on by Dee Ford and Don Gardner called *I Need Your Lovin'* and from that point I became fond of the Blues." Chicago Beau was ten.

One day Beau and childhood friend, Julio Finn, went down to the Blue Flame Lounge where Julio's brother, Billy Boy Arnold, was playing. Beau said, "He showed me a few licks on the harp then I continued to pursue the Blues."

When asked what kept him moving so much he said, "It's the creative spirit that keeps you going. The world becomes an avenue that is just one of the tributaries that I have a pass to walk down. Some people wait for opportunities to knock on their door not me. I knock the door down. I have always been that way. I was so used to people being very cordial over in Europe; here was just the opposite. At that point I flipped a coin to see if I was going to go to San Francisco or go back to New York. Heads was New York, and tails was San Francisco. Tails won, but before I went to San Francisco I stopped in Chicago to see my parents for three days. While at home, I hit a few of my old hangouts and much to my surprise many of them were gone. It made me so sad to see the plight of my people when I went down to 47th Street. Toronato's and Silvio's on the West side were gone.

I'll be glad if Black folks get together and collectively fix up the South side. 47th Street was *Downtown* for Black folks because we weren't allowed Downtown. We had everything we ever needed right here on 47th Street."

J.W. Williams

"I've got the Blues not because my woman left, but because she came back." J.W. sang in church as a boy in Magnolia, Mississippi. "I came to Chicago," he said, "in 1962, and formed the Castels and started playing a variety of music . . . a little bit of Rock & Roll, and a little bit of Blues. In the later part of the '60s, I started getting into Rhythm & Blues and kind of a Hard Rock thing."

In 1976, he formed the Chi-Town Hustlers. "I love my Blues and I'm glad to see more young Black people getting into it. This is what I would like to see more of even if they might do it in a different fashion."

The most memorable moment in his career came when his beloved mother came to a show of his at Mothers Lounge at 2500 East 79th Street. He said, "This was the best feeling I had in my life when my mom came to the set. My mother came in and I was singing and she hollered out, 'Baby, don't you sing too hard. You're gonna hurt yourself.' Tears started coming down my face and I kept on [singing]. My mother walked up to me and took the microphone. She said, 'Baby, you're working too hard.' I felt so good [that] I could hardly play. I was all choked up just to have my mom there. It felt so good to know that she was just that concerned about me. That was the best moment for me, as far as playing in my whole life. I felt like I was on top of the world."

Flavio Guimaraes

Flavio Guimaraes of Rio de Janeiro, Brazil and I met on August 27, 1988 at Rosa's during a Sugar Blue performance. He came to Chicago to play and study the Blues.

I invited Flavio to my family cook-out on September 4th. The cook-out turned into a jam session. Chicago Beau, Joe Mascolino, J.W. Williams, comedian Martin "Uncle Marty" Hunter, and my brothers, Foree and Greg, were among the house rockers. This interview with Flavio took place outside Rosa's September 9, 1988 at 1:00 AM:

> *FJ: What made you come to Chicago?*
> *FG: I came to Chicago because I have records that were recorded in Chicago and I always Wanted to come.*

FJ: Are records very expensive due to importation?
FG: They are expensive, $20. You put them in cruzeiros (Brazilian currency) it costs a lot. Usually, I record them on tape.
FJ: Did you think twice about coming?
FG: Not really.
FJ: Was this your first time here?
FG: No, I came here when I was fifteen years old. I don't remember that time very well, but I liked it. I went to high school in Indiana and I lived with an American family in an exchange program. It was very nice.
FJ: How long did you plan for this trip?
FG: Two years.
FJ: Is this trip expensive?
FG: It's very expensive. Maybe I would like to come back here every year, but I probably won't have the chance again very soon, If our band, Blues Etilicos, goes better maybe I'll have money to come back here next year.
FJ: Who did you come to Chicago to learn from?
FG: I met Sugar Blue last year in Rio (when he was on tour with Buddy Guy). I think I'm learning a lot from him. I came to learn mostly harmonica. Listening to his shows ... he's very nice. Howard Levy also taught me some harmonica.
FJ: What did your parents say when you told them that you wanted to come here?
FG: My parents helped me. My father made this trip possible.

Carl Weathersby

Carl Weathersby is from Mississippi, and the grandson of Downhome Bluesman Allen Weathersby. His grandfather's guitar playing influenced him most. "Living with him exposed me to Blues music." Carl said, "because during that time in Mississippi Blues was the most powerful music around. Like kids now listen to L.L. Cool J and Kool Moe D and all of those guys, I grew up listening to Howlin' Wolf and Muddy Waters. I learned Blues first, and then I moved North with my mother and father. That's when I finally became aware of the Temptations and the Soul music flavor that was out. First of all, try to play the Blues and then add something to it. That's the technique I use. Coming from the Blues, my grandfather always told me that if you could play the Blues, and play it fairly well, you wouldn't have any problem playing anything else."

FJ: Why do you feel young Blacks don't seem get as involved in the Blues as much as other youths do?
CW: The Blues was around then it disappeared from the mainstream stations like WGCI and WBMX. They played the Blues up until around 1972/73. After Albert King had I'll Play the Blues for You, [you] didn't hear too much Blues on the radio anywhere. Every now a then you'd hear the giants like Bobby Bland and B.B. King. Even Little Milton suffered from not getting air-play.

76

We traveled to some of the far corners of the earth in some of the most unlikely places like Nicaragua, Bolivia, Chile, Ghana, and they have heard of Eric Clapton and Stevie Ray Vaughan, but they have never heard of B.B. King or Albert King. A guy stopped me in a sound check in Dominica and said, "Hey man, that's an Eric Clapton song." I said, 'No, no, no. That's an Albert King song [Born Under a Bad Sign]. Albert did it in 1964 and Clapton copied it.' But they don't know. A lot of the people have ideas of how the Blues should be. You can dress it up, but if it doesn't have that gut-wrenching wind to it, it's not Blues. It's the most simplistic form of music that you can play because it's only three chords. It's the way you put those flavors and feelings in there. It's hard to do that in any other styles of music. It's a song of sadness and joy.

Robert "Bob" Stroger

FJ: When you first started out playing did you think that it would grow to this magnitude?
RS: Not really. When I started out it was just for fun. I was playing just to be playing. [I] never meant to make a living at it. I just wanted to be able to play. I enjoyed playing.
FJ: This makes it seem like your living hasn't been in vain.
RS: That's right! And the way that I feel about it now is that I'm leaving a mark. I have got far enough that people will remember me when I'm dead and gone. That's the mark that younger bass players will come along and see what the Blues is all about; not to get rich at it, but it's good to make a living at it.
FJ: How do you feel when you see that young Blacks are trying to preserve the music?
RS: I feel really good when guys claim their roots. A lot of guys "get up" and forget about it. When I see the younger guys on the street I try to give them all of the encouragement that I can.

Dave Myers

FJ: Who were some of the people you played and recorded with?
DM: Little Walter, Big Boy Crudop, Muddy Waters, Howlin' Wolf, Big Joe Williams, Lonnie Brooks, the Fabulous Faith Gospel Group, Junior Wells, my brother [Louis Myers], Earl Hooker, Snooky Pryor, Sunnyland Slim, man, and so many more.
FJ: Tell me the story of how Little Walter hooked up with y'all.
DM: Well, Junior Wells was playing harp with us at the time and Walter was playing with Muddy [Waters]. That's around the time when Walter had Juke out and it was hittin' all over, man. Anyway, Muddy and Walter had a disagreement. You know how that goes. Walter wanted to play Juke and Muddy wouldn't let him. So, one night we were at a gig and we were waiting around for Junior to show up. After a while, we saw Walter standing by the bar. We knew that he was supposed to be on the road with Mud, so I asked him why was he there. Since Junior didn't show up he came up and played.
FJ: What happened to Junior?
DM: He went with Muddy.
FJ: So, what happened?

DM: When we played on the road with Walter we were called Little Walter and the Jukes.
FJ: Who was in the band?
DM: Little Walter, Louis [Myers], Fred Below, and me.
FJ: What was the band called before Junior Wells left?
DM: We were called the Four Aces. And before we had Junior we were called the Three Deuces. When I tell you this, I know you are gonna laugh. When people used to see us coming to play they used to say, "Here they come. Here come the Little Boys."

Carlos Johnson

FJ: Where do you see the future of the Blues headed?
CJ: I see it going way up. Especially with the Blue-Bloods out here making it in the cross over market, and changing the old concept of it being an 'old fogy' music. It never has been in the first place, but it had been thought of that way. Now you've got a lot of young cats and girls coming up with the Blues and they have a fresh new approach and I think they are going to do very well.
FJ: What keeps you playing?
CJ: It's the only music that hits me from my butt to my heart. It's a soul felt music. I don't play it because I can read it, I play it because I feel it. That's why I'm sticking with it. I know it's genuine.

George McNairy

When I interviewed my uncle, George, about the clubs back in the good old days he said, "Club DeLisa used to be on the ball. They had shows there like they have in New York. They had chorus girls on stage. You'd pay $1 to get in and $1 for a set-up (a spirited drink with a side order of ice). You and your girlfriend could go there with $5 and see a good show. The Club DeLisa and places like that--people would be lined up outside waiting to get in. We had nightclubs! They don't have nothing now. The clubs that we do have, have been pushed up North to the White sections.

"There was a time, man, that we had night clubs all over Chicago, all up and down 63rd Street. It was on the ball. There was a time in the late ĕ5 when Blacks would 'chin the moon' to get a chance to go to Hyde Park [High School] because it was a high rated school and it was predominately White."

Uncle George frequented the Sutherland Hotel on 47th & Drexel as a music fan when he lived on 43rd & Drexel. "Dinah Washington and all of 'em would be there. We wouldn't be able to get in t re for the White people coming back over there. You know they were moving out the area and Blacks were moving in, but they were coming back for the shows. The Sutherland [Hotel] was on the ball!" Bobby Bland, Little Junior Parker, and Muddy Waters were a few of the acts my uncle saw at the Sutherland Hotel. "I've seen the time when we'd line up for two or three blocks to get into the Regal Theater. I remember, I used to go there and see Sammy Davis, Jr., his uncle and his father, Pearl Bailey and her husband [Louie Bellson], her brother, and Sam Cooke."

Manuel Arrington

Manuel was a member of the Electric Crazy People on WVON AM 1390 in the early '80s. This interview was done backstage at the Chicago Blues Fest on June 10, 1989.

> *MA: Well, Fernando, how ya doin'? How are you feeling today? Are you enjoying yourself? Man, this has got to be the greatest event in the world as far as I'm concerned. What do you think?*
> *FJ: How do you feel about young Blacks preserving the Blues?*
> *MA: I love it! I love it man. Guys your age will preserve Blues for the next one million and one years.*

The Black Lone Ranger

FJ: How did you get started?
BLR: I started out with Muddy Waters back in the 1950s and I've been puttin' it on. And I've been riding the trail ever since.
FJ: How do you tie that into your act?
BLR: During the time when I came to Chicago I got hooked up with Muddy. I was doing gun tricks, stunts, and Blues singing. When the Texas Rangers got killed, and Dan Reeves, who was the real Lone Ranger got killed, I became the Legend of the Lone Ranger.
FJ: Have you ever talked to any of those people?
BLR: I talked to Clayton Moore word to word.
FJ: How does this tie in with the Blues?
BLR: Well, Muddy Waters taught me to blow all of the Blues that I know, and I'm still singing the legend of the Blues, and I don't think that I'm ready to retire yet. So now I'm gonna sign off. HI-OH-SILVER AWAY!!!

Street Performers

When I was about eight or nine years old my brother, Greg, used to take me to see movies Downtown by way of the L-train. Sometimes we would ride from 59th & Wentworth, but most of the time we'd catch the train on 59th & State Street. Mr. Gray's barber shop was right next to the L-stop on State. Usually, we'd ride the train to the Jackson stop Downtown. I'd cling to the subway walls because my parents had warned me about the third rail and how it could electrocute you if you touched it. The trains were loud and squeaky in the subway. That madness made my flesh crawl.

Now, some thirty years later, I still travel byway of the Chicago Transit Authority's (CTA) L-trains Downtown from time to time. The once drab, lackluster subway that I remember from childhood have now transformed itself into forums for some of Chicago's most ambitious and talented entertainers. The subway platforms, in particular, serve as stages with built in audiences for singers, musicians, visual artists, and dancers.

One of the best acts playing on the *street* in the late '80s was the Ultimate Vocal & Image Group of which featured Malik on upright bass-fiddle, his older brother, Cephus, played twelve string guitar and sang lead, their sister Makeda sang background, and a friend, Ron, sang co-lead. They were regularly seen on Michigan Avenue in front of the Water Tower Place.

Darrell "Creasebone" Creasy is a professional trombone player who performs along side many of the city's top performers. This is how he and his fellow horn players got started playing on the *street*: "One summer when we were playing with Little Milton [Campbell], and we were off the road back in Chicago it was me, Garrick, this guy named Steve Maynard, and Johnny Cotton (now playing with the Ohio Players). We didn't have a drummer or anything.

"During the day we played while on tour with Little Milton in Shreveport, Louisiana for about twenty minutes, just jammin'. We were just playing to soothe our own souls—this was about '83 . . . next thing when we'd look up and there would be money in our cases. Right now it's kind of messed up for us. We [Creasebone, Garrick, Mozak, the late James 'Om Phop Amadrig Omega' Lockett, and Boney] were the first to get permits to play Downtown. It's different in Canada. Their thing is, you have to audition to be able to play in the subway. Playing in their subways is like being in the Union [the American Federation of Musicians] here."

Garrick, Mozak, and Creasebone played on State Street between Carson Pirie Scott's and Marshall Field's during the Christmas season of '85. A week or so later, I met and befriended tap dancer Ayrie "Mr. Taps" King III in front of Carson's. He danced to pre-recorded tracks with his four year old Godson, Freddie. There were also young Black and Hispanic break dancers Downtown performing on the street corners, too.

> *Blood from my fingertips bathe the frets as I baptize my new creation.*
> *I change with the wind and I change with the time*
> *Never have to buy or sell because everything is mine.*

S E V E N
Blues as a Second Language

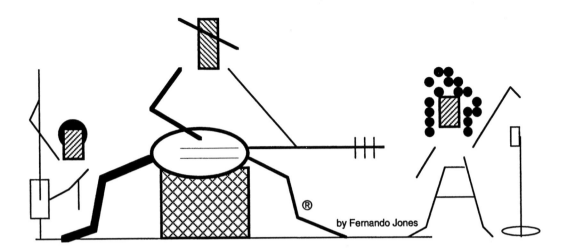

by Fernando Jones

American History can't be taught honestly without talking about the African American's artistic and cultural contributions to it. And that story can't be taught without talking about the Blues. Can you dig that? The Blues is as American as baseball, hotdogs, apple pie, and Chevrolet.

Wouldn't it be fantastic if the Blues could be taught in classrooms throughout the United States and infused into daily lesson plans? Yes. This art form is a treasure chest filled with the dreams, hopes, aspirations, and accomplishments of people set to, but not limited to music. Studying history through the lens of the Blues can be fun and exciting. Fernando Jones' Blues Kids of America, Ltd. is a multicultural, interdisciplinary arts-in-education music program.

Our goal is for primary and secondary students to be able to recognize, appreciate, and perform this music in safe, user friendly environments such as classrooms, museums, music halls, etcetera, at a world class level.

The objective is to introduce this indigenous African American art form and culture in a hands-on setting to students throughout the country, while infusing Geography, History, Language Arts, Drama, and Mathematics. Students will learn to express themselves through their respective instruments at their own pace and level.

In this section, you'll hear from some students who think learning about the Blues in school is fantastic. Students involved in my Blues Kids of America program, for example, have found it to be an informative, inspirational, entertaining, and educational experience.

"Blues for a New Generation" by Jeff Johnson
Chicago Sun-Times • Sunday, February 2, 2003

Fernando Jones calls himself "a 24-hour-a-day Bluesman," but he's as passionate about teaching the Blues as he is about playing them.

Jones works as a language arts teacher on the Southwest Side, where he informally continues his Blues Kids of America curriculum, which he has been offering for more than a decade in the schools. Seven to 10 kids, armed with harmonicas, drums and whatever additional instruments Jones can scrounge, learn the Blues from the working Blues guitarist-vocalist after school.

"I got a chance to be involved with the Blues as a youth, and now this is my way of giving back to kids in the inner city," Jones says.

The Blues musician and educator is a renaissance man, as well. He has dabbled as a composer, author, historian, filmmaker, illustrator, poet and playwright. He also has received accolades for his acting, including a Jeff Citation for his supporting role as a blind man in "Lifting."

You can add role model to that list as well. Children in serious need of a father figure greet their confident, capable, well-dressed teacher in the hallway with eyes filled with admiration and affection.

Some of the kids, like sixth-graders Cleveland Bell and Anthony Brown, have family members who sing or play an instrument.

"My mom likes to sing in church," says Anthony, echoing the background of many an aspiring Bluesman. "When they told us we'd get to play music [in Jones' program], I wanted to try it so I can learn the harmonica and be famous someday."

Jermond Sharkey, 11, is taking up the harmonica. But besides the joy of learning an instrument, Jermond says he appreciates learning more about the history and background of the music. "I liked when we heard about other people who played the harmonica and Blues," he says.

Jones has been commanding that same level of respect in the Chicago Public Schools ever since his early '90s stint at Ella Flagg Young Elementary on the hardscrabble West Side, when he would lead his makeshift Blues bands of 30 or more members in all-school assemblies.

With electives missing from the curriculum at many cash-strapped public schools, Jones maintains that many children are growing up without even a fundamental understanding of music.

"So many kids listen to Rap and other music and have no idea what instrumentation is," he says. "The only time they might hear real instruments is if they go to church.

While Jones is unaware of any former program participants pursuing Blues or other music seriously, he says, "With all the harmonicas I've given away over the years, I wouldn't be surprised."

Teacher and pupils will be appearing in an all-ages program Feb. 27 at the DuSable Museum of African-American History. In addition to a performance by Jones' Blues band, called My Band, he'll proudly introduce some of his young Blues artists in training.

Superintendent Dr. Essie Harris from the Riverdale, Illinois Public School District had this to say in defense of this music and culture being implemented in the classroom: "The Blues is another form of music. And if we teach music and music appreciation in our elementary schools as well as high schools, and universities, I think that the best place to get started would be at the elementary level because little people are so responsive to rhythm, and sound, and words."

> Stay in School Blues
> by Fernando Jones
> ©1994
> Bluefunkjazroll Music, BMI
>
> I'm gonna stay in school. (4x)
> I'm gonna stay in school
> Because the world doesn't need one more fool.
>
> I'm gonna do my work. (4x)
> I'm gonna do my work
> Because success doesn't hurt.
> I'm gonna do my work!
>
> I'm gonna do my best. (4x)
> I'm gonna do my best
> And pass any test.
> I'm gonna do my best!
> Vas a quedar en la escuela. (4x)
> I'm gonna stay in school
> Because the world doesn't need one more fool!

Chicago Public School administrator Will Stigall said, "The Blues should be a required part of the educational system for all students. It is a sociological medicine for many, myself included. When I feel down and put on the Blues it brings me back."

Dr. Frank Adams had this to say in relationship to the importance of music education: "Young Black people, or young people of any race should drink deeply of the Blues because of its feeling, and because of its structure. We find out that a learning of the Blues is an introduction to other forms and can be used to teach subjects that may not be directly related to Blues. It's so critical that young Black people, or any group of people that have been in bondage, should know their history. They should know the very cultural things that they have contributed as a race to civilization. And you must realize that the Blues were most likely sung during the years of slavery. You can take the songs, the spirituals all are based somewhat on a Blues feeling and also Blues structure.

"When you think of music and art of any kind there is a mathematical dimension and there's a linguistic dimension. The Blues basically consists of twelve measures of music, and that can be broken down into very small components, and when one learns the music, or how to perform, or talk in the style of the Blues then we get into measured time. For instance, we can measure our heartbeat to a rhythm. And we can measure the Blues and its structure and it gives us a sense of where we are, this gives us a sense of time. And we teach this to people, they can be young or they can be old, but the fundamental thing is there.

'It's something that's inherently felt. For example, we can take a meter in music and we can say that this is a certain number of beats, or a certain number of pulses in a certain rhythm. And we can create language, we can create expression within that form, and this is when all of the subjects interact—English, Spelling, Math, and History. Those kind of things can be understood and broken down into a Blues pattern.

"Within a form we can create, we can be inspired to paint, to express all types of emotions in the Blues. Once, it was thought that the Blues represented somethin' sad, but musicians have demonstrated world wide, particularly, Blues players, that the music could be happy, it could be sad, and can run a gamut of all emotions in between."

Playwright Okoro Harold Johnson said, "First of all, we must control the promotion and proliferation of the Blues and all of our creativity. Secondly, we must always present our music to our future generation in a positive manner, letting them know the truth of it's creation. Thirdly, we must encourage teachers, musicians, ministers and other leaders to educate and perpetuate the true knowledge of our culture and creativity."

When Jerry "Boogie" McCain in Birmingham, Alabama was asked about the importance of this music being taught in schools he said, "Jerry 'Boogie' McCain is the real thing. Live in person and living color, baby. Briefly, I started playing the harmonica when I was five years old, I'm sixty-eight, now. I've been playin' for sixty-three years. I also play the harmonica with my nose. No brag just facts. My mother played guitar in the church. My aunt played guitar in church. My mother could play guitar and tune it. My aunt could play it and couldn't tune it. I could tune it and couldn't play it." Then he laughed and said, "That's the way things happen."

"It is very important to play and practice and especially in my position and condition. When I was buying harmonicas at that time they were 25¢, but they don't cost that now. They cost much more. It is important to practice because I didn't have any lessons. I wasn't taught by anyone to play the harmonica. God gave me my talent. You can't even steal it, I won't sell it, and you can't take it away. If you practice and play harmonica [you have to] practice, practice, practice because practice makes perfect.

"There are people goin' around teaching people how to play the harmonica now, but when I was coming up there were no teachers. I just had to listen to the record player [and] crank it up like you do an old A-Model, or T-Model Ford. If the kids, especially the Black kids, don't get out there and start playing Blues they lose. Our culture is gone. Somebody else is doin' it. You understand where I'm comin' from? There's a whole lot of copying goin' on . . . somebody sound like somebody else, and these kids gotta get off this Rap and stop messin' with this crap and do some Blues. They're gonna have to do that because we'll lose a culture, but it's goin' down the drain if we don't do a thang."

Dr. Jimmy Tillman said, "Our [Black] kids now have left this all together. Our music is collecting dust. We are now trying to bring Blues to students in schools. Our children may wind up shouting and screaming to blond hair, blue eyed Blues singers, and may never play it again because they may think that the only people that can play the Blues have to be White people."

Science teacher and Rapper Ty "Grand Hank" Raggsdale of Philadelphia said, "Rap music to me is a key factor in helping students to want to learn what they need to know. Students love Rap and they listen to it all the time, but the Rap music they listen to doesn't necessarily translate to the information that they need to succeed. I think its a vital component they listen to it everyday, and not only do they listen, they retain.

"What we do is package useful information into the music so that they are not just getting a Rap song about a story about how, for example, *the streets are so tough* and *you need to carry guns* and *be a big baller* and all that. What I'm trying to help them understand is that you can use that same music to teach about Physics, to teach Chemistry, to teach Math, to teach English, and Communications."

Dr. Fannie Gibson
Retired Chicago Public School Principal
and Chicago Area Alliance of Black School Educators, President

The Blues is an important part or our history. There's a lot of research that has shown that music and the arts are extremely important in helping to develop reading, in particular, for children in the inner city.

Rashawna Guy a.k.a. Shawna
of the Rap group Disturbing Tha Peace
and daughter of legendary Bluesman Buddy Guy

Well, the Blues, for one, has been a major influence [in my life] sine I was born. Being the only thing that my dad wanted to do, he just wanted to play the guitar for people to hear and write his music. And now that I'm growing more in the industry, I see that that's my same goal—is just to let people hear my talent and write my music.

I think the Blues is an important form of music for African Americans because of the expressions and the emotions in the music. It's a way for us to come together and express ourselves. It makes you feel better when it's done.

Lana Cromwell, ESL Specialist
Harriet Tubman School, College Park, GA

My kids became very interested in the history of [Blues] music. They had a greater appreciation for the different genres of music. They were very much enthralled with Mr. Jones, himself, as a Black male and role model. My class had a great deal of admiration for Mr. Jones. They were very eager to learn to play an instrument [harmonica]. Anything after that certainly increased their awareness of music, and certainly enhanced their motivation to do better in their courses of band, orchestra, and chorus.

Fred Donkor, Music Teacher
Carleton Heights Public School, Ottawa, Ontario

The Blues mean sharing a lot of history. Without the Blues we don't have contemporary music. I think providing Blues in the Schools actually provides students with a well-rounded musical education opposed one particular style.

On Friday, November 21, 1998 we had an impromptu discussion on this subject in the lobby of the Town and Country Hotel in San Diego, California during the National Alliance of Black School Educators Conference with educators Oadie Carter, Angela Chapman, Bridgette Pronty, and G. Seporia Holland-Wilson.

Educators who have had the Blues Kids experience

Angela Chapman
Coventry Elementary School in Cleveland Heights, Ohio
The audience was definitely actively involved in the presentation. They were kind of sad when it was over. They wanted more. It was also a time for the participants in the audience to get to know each other, and in some ways fellowship. At the same time, they were learning about part of their history and their culture, and about famous Blues musicians.

I think anyone who attended the workshop, or presentation would have a lot to take back to their building, or district to share with their colleagues. I was thoroughly impressed with the presentation.

Bridgette Pronty
Carylwood Intermediate School in Bedford, Ohio
I don't know too much about the Blues, but from what I do know I think it would be positive to educate students with it because it is part of our African American culture. So anything that would help us in the classroom that's from our heritage and our background is positive.

Oadie Carter
Chicago Area Alliance of Black School Educators Officer
The Blues is our heritage and if we don't pass it down it will be lost totally. It's ours to pass down. If we don't pass it down and somebody else passes it down the original Blues is lost forever

G. Seporia Holland-Wilson
National Alliance of Black School Educators, Richmond, Virginia
From a teaching perspective it gives creativity and another way of introducing information in which ordinarily students would find boring because it's history, and it's the past. And they are not familiar with the past so they find it difficult addressing it and thinking of it as culture so I think it's significant to use the Blues in teaching other areas.

1998 Teachers • Birmingham, Alabama

Avon Nelson
Glenn Middle School Teacher

The importance of Blues in the Schools has been a very enriching program for our students. I've been in the program since it started in Birmingham and I've found that with this program it has inspired our children to do a little bit more and [has] built self-esteem up increasingly. I've noticed some wonderful things just being part of Blues in the Schools. I know that the students have really thoroughly enjoyed the program because they can't wait for the Blues in the Schools bus to come.

Susan Parks
Banks Middle School Teacher

This is a very rewarding program. I have been With it since it's inception. It offers a very valuable outlet to our inner city students. It also raises the self-esteem because that is a problem with our inner city students.

Melva Folks
Glenn Middle School Teacher

Blues in the Schools has helped our kids to enhance a lot of their self-esteem. They've had an opportunity to go out and experience the musical field and get exposed to how other cultures conduct themselves, and I feel this program has really helped our inner city kids.

Broderick Canada
Curby Middle School Teacher

Programs like this help kids because it brings kids from other schools together, and it gives them the chance to intermingle with each another. It teaches discipline and it educates them to present things that are gonna be happening in music as well as things that have happened in the past.

We have people right here in Alabama who have made important contributions to Blues and other types of music that our kids are not aware of because they listen to the radio all the time. They have to find out where this music comes from before they can find out where it's goin'. Blues in the Schools has been a very good program and it has taught the kids discipline and has brought, like I said, kids closer from different schools.

1998 Blues Kids in Birmingham, Alabama

Hermeka: 8th Grade, Curby Middle School
I think Blues in the Schools is a great experience for us, and I like it.

Faytesia: 6th Grade, Glenn Middle School
Blues in the Schools has helped me with a lot of history, and it brought me together with more friends and different stuff like that. Blues in the Schools is really fun. I hope to be in it next year.

Ife: 7th Grade, Banks Middle School
Blues in the Schools taught me more songs, and I made more friends. I hope I can attend next year, and I hope other people can attend it, too.

LaToya: 8th Grade, Curby Middle School
I enjoyed being in Blues in the Schools even though this was my last year.

•

2002 Lanier High School Teachers • Jackson, Mississippi

Anne Johnson, English Teacher
The Blues is a feeling. It's a feeling. Sometimes it sad. Sometimes it's happy. The Blues to me carries an emotion of a people. So, I think about our people when they did write songs they were expressing their emotions. Whether it was talking about a loved one, or someone they wanted to meet. So it's an emotion, an expression: Good, bad, or could sometimes be joyous.

Gladys Sykes
Retired English Teacher
I love the Blues! I think the Blues was born out of oppression, sadness and a feeling of not being able to do what you wanted to do or accomplish.

Jolivette Anderson
Arts-in-Education Consultant
The Blues is the heart and the soul of my people. The Blues is something that is tangible. You can hear it, taste it, smell it, touch it, and feel it. The Blues is Blackness. The Blues is black that is so black that it's blue.

•

Fernando Jones

2002 Lanier High School Students • Jackson, Mississippi

Robin Smith, 12th Grade
To me the Blues is basically telling a story of deep dark feelings within.

Rickedra Martin, 11th Grade
Blues is an expression of the body, mind, and soul through words with a beat.

Kenyatta Cleark, 12th Grade
The Blues is music that people can relate to. It's not necessarily a music that'll probably make you feel down or bad. I think that in order for people to understand that there is someone that might be goin' through the same thing they are goin' through.

Jordan Jackson, 12th Grade
I believe that Blues is just music that you can feel; music that you can relate to.

Ashley Haralson, 11th Grade
The Blues is what makes misery or what makes you feel bad or situations that brought upon failure and sadness to your life.

Janna Hughes, 12th Grade
I feel that the Blues is a passionate form of music that goes deeply into the roots of African Americans, not only African Americans but other races and it tells a story. I feel that the Blues tells a story about the past, present, and also future.

•

1999 Undergraduate students from Dr. Lily Golden's
African American Studies Fall class at Chicago State University

Denise Duncan
The Blues depicts a part of our rich culture. I grew up around my father and other relatives who loved B.B. King and Bobby "Blue" Bland. I believe that the Blues is an expression of our many experiences as a people.

Anita Miles
I love the Blues. It has a good beat. Somehow it touches the inner you.

90

Derek P. Smith

The Blues to me is the reaction to an action called institutionalized racism. It is also the changing of a bad thing to good.

Tony Horton

Blues to me is when the extrinsic shallow doors of a person's persona closes, and the intrinsic doors of a person's soul pours out the truth—clear, cut, and dry. The simplicity of Blues music is an art within itself.

Theresa Fletcher

My opinion of Blues has always been that Blues is sad, dark, and depressing. I had no knowledge of the rich history Blues has, nor the influence it has had on all other music styles. I am more interested now after hearing you [Fernando Jones] speak today than I ever had been.

•

You can't play the Blues
Until you lose
The only thang you never thought
You'd ever lose.
We play the Blues because we have to.

Something from Fernando

If you decide to use or reproduce my songs for whatever reasons please credit them properly.

Oil & Water
by Fernando Jones 2/19/00
Recorded by Nellie Travis
©2000
Bluefunkjazroll Music, BMI

You remind me of a hurricane,
But you treat me like a candle in the rain.
I give you money, give you my time
But I know you'll never be mine.
I've tried all of the tricks, still,
Oil and water don't mix.

I just remembered I don't know your name.
Is it Billy the Kid or Jesse James?
You're so fine, but you treat me oh so mean.
I've tried all of the tricks, still,
Oil and water don't mix.
    If I was a bottle of glue still I couldn't stick to you.
    I might as well be a brick wall because you never call.
    I've tried all of the tricks, still,
    Oil and water don't mix.

You remind me of a hurricane,
But you treat me like a candle in the rain.
I give you money, give you my time
But I know you'll never be mine.
I've tried all of the tricks, still,
Oil and water don't mix.

On Top
by Fernando Jones 4/17/99
Recorded by Foree Superstar
©1999
Bluefunkjazroll Music, BMI

I should of never gave you my heart.
[I] Should of known better right from the start.
I never thought I'd see the day
You'd turn your back on me.
     When you're on the bottom, and I'm on top.
     I ain't gonna love you no mo' [but] right now, I cain't stop.

Every day's a new day for everybody else.
Today's a blue day you got somebody else.
Cain't have a conversation without bringin' up your name.
On a sunny day all I see is rain.
     When you're on the bottom, and I'm on top.
     I ain't gonna love you no mo' [but] right now, I cain't stop.

Mama's baby boy. Come on with it Fernando.
Get on down. That's what I'm talkin' 'bout . . . Blues time. Hey!

You put me out with no place to go.
You put me out with 4 feet of snow.
Mama said put you out.
Papa said send you back down South.
     When you're on the bottom, and I'm on top.
     I ain't gonna love you no mo' [but] right now, I cain't stop.

Nefertiti
by Fernando Jones 7/3/01
©2001
Bluefunkjazroll Music, BMI

Could-Egypt have existed without, without, with/out you?
A promised land of / earth, water, and air.
God's gift to you.

Pyramid pillows, and sand / for grass . . . at last
You are everlasting.
Your profile we see enchanting memory
In time, in mind.

Paper-sack tan face carved in, limestone,
Alone
For me so true.
Beautiful profile.
Can you look at [me] as I do you?

I've only seen the side of your, your face
The face of you in my mind
What is it that has made forever,
You smile. Profile?

Love not war
Is what God created you for
Cleo [Cleopatra] was cool
[But] had nothing on you
Supreme-being.

Could-Egypt have existed without, without, with/out you?
A promised land of / earth, water, and air.
God's gift to you.

Is Somethin' Wrong With My English
by Fernando Jones 5/7/01
Written for my Japanese Blues brutha, Shun
©2001
Bluefunkjazroll Music, BMI

I treat you like a queen
You treat me not so nice
Still I love you with all my heart.

When I'm with you
You're cold as ice
Still, I don't want us to be apart.
　　　I love you.
　　　Don't you understand this?
　　　Baby, is there somethin' wrong with my English?

I put food on your plate,
And keep none for myself.

All I want is for you to see
That for you, I'm the best.
　　　Woman, I love you.
　　　Don't you understand this?
　　　Baby, is there somethin' wrong with my English?

Sometimes I feel like leavin' you alone
Just walk away from our brand new home.

But sometimes I think you just might care
Then I change my mind, and hang on in there.
　　　Woman, I love you.
　　　Don't you understand this?
　　　Baby, is there somethin' wrong with my English?

Everybody Knows
by Fernando Jones 12/9/00
Recorded by Marylin Claire
©2000
Bluefunkjazroll Music, BMI

Everybody knows that I don't like to drink,
But if you were a spirit.
I'd get drunk . . . don't care what the people . . .
Thinkin' of you, makes me smile
Thinkin' of you, I'm happy as a child.
        (Talk) That's why I don't drink!

Everybody knows that I don't get high
But if you were a drug, I'd be curious enough to give you a . . .
Trying so hard to get you off my mind.
I can't sleep at night cuz you're so fine.
        (Talk) Now, [do you] wonder why I don't get high?

Everybody knows that I don't smoke, and that's the law.
But if you were a square I'd have to take a . . .
Drawing picture all day of me and you.
Together like we're in grade 2.
        (Talk) Thank God I don't smoke.

Everybody knows that I don't like to drink,
But if you were a spirit.
I'd get drunk . . . don't care what the people . . .
Thinkin' of you, makes me smile
Thinkin' of you, I'm happy as a child.
        (Talk) That's why I don't drink!

Dime & A Quarter
by Fernando Jones 2/13/00
Recorded by Nellie Travis on the "I Got It Like That" CD
©2000
Bluefunkjazroll Music, BMI

If you like me, [well then] like me.
If you need me, baby, need me.
If you want me, baby, want me all night long.
　　Here's a dime and a quarter.
　　Call me on the telephone.

If you love me, baby, love me.
If you hug me, baby, you gotta hug me.
Because if you want me, baby,
You've gotta want me all night long.
　　Here's a dime and quarter.
　　Call me on the telephone.

If you hold my hand I want you to understand
That I'm not your typical . . . woooh!
Becaues if you want me, baby,
You've gotta want me all night long.
　　Here's a dime and quarter.
　　Call me on the telephone.

If you like me, [well then] like me.
If you need me, baby, need me.
If you want me, baby, want me all night long.
　　Here's a dime and a quarter.
　　Call me on the telephone.

Tracee
by Fernando Jones 1/29/02
©2002
Bluefunkjazroll Music, BMI
*Inspired by Lana

Sometimes she forgets she's beautiful.
One look in her amber eyes and see pure soul.
One day it'll hit her what she means to me.
She makes me more than by myself I could ever be.
     Tracee, I'm cra-zee '
     Cra-zee 'bout you.

Blushing face in her hands on a long distance call.
[She] opens a parceled sent from a man she barely knows at all.
She says, "I haven't gotten you anything."
You've taught me how to love unconditionally.
     Tracee, I'm cra-zee '
     Cra-zee 'bout you.
     Cra-zee 'bout you. Tracee, I'm cra-zee '

When I first met you I looked deep into you smile.
Never wanting to exploit you
Just wanted to make you mine.
Three years later in November, on a California Saturday night
I knew then and there that I wanted you honorably in my life.
Tracee, I'm cra-zee '
Cra-zee 'bout you.

Love at first sight.
Love you, I do.

Nothin's Greater Than Love
Alternate Title: Somethin' Special
by Fernando Jones 2/12/00
Recorded by Nellie Travis on the "I Got It Like That" CD
©2000
Bluefunkjazroll Music, BMI

Introduction: Sometimes we try so hard to be the best at whatever it is that we're doin', and so many times we forget the little things . . . the little things like calling your family, or your best friends, but all I have to say is

If never I see you again doesn't mean we're not friends.
If never I see your face doesn't mean someone has taken your place.
We have somethin' special from above and nothin's greater than love.
We have somethin' special from above and nothin's greater than love.
La-la-la luh-la-la-la
La-la-la woooh, Woooh

La-la-la luh-la-la-la
La-la-la woooh, Woooh

If I don't call you for a while, and if I stop comin' 'round
No matter where I am I want you to know that I ain't put you down
We have somethin' special from above and nothin's greater than love.
We have somethin' special from above and nothin's greater than love.
We have somethin' special from above and nothin's greater than love.
We have somethin' special from above and nothin's greater than love.

I'm In Love With A Blues Man
by Fernando Jones 3/93
Recorded by Shiri Riley
©1993
Bluefunkjazroll Music, BMI

Doo doo doo
       Doo doo doo doo doo doo
Doo doo doo
       Doo doo doo doo doo doo
Mama, I'm in love with a Bluesman.
Don't try and understand.
He stays out all night,
And he ain't got a nine to five,
But he treats her nice.
       Mama, I'm in love with a Bluesman . . .
       Mama, I'm in love with a Bluesman . . .
       A Bluesman.
       A Bluesman.

In 12 bars he seduces me.
In every key unloosens me.
I know he loves me
And you might not approve
Of me and the man of Blues.
       Mama, I'm in love with a Bluesman . . .
       Mama, I'm in love with a Bluesman . . .
       A Bluesman.
       A Bluesman.

       A lament for me he never plays.
       His love for me is all I crave.
       He's my everything and all I need
       I'm in love, mama, can't you see.
           Mama, I'm in love with a Bluesman . . .
           Mama, I'm in love with a Bluesman . . .
           A Bluesman.
       A Bluesman.

Smoke filled rooms is all he knows.
He wears his hats ace-deuce and loud color clothes.
He's got a mouth like a sailor.
But he treats me like an angel.
When we're together, I'm all that matters.
       Mama, I'm in love with a Bluesman . . .
       Mama, I'm in love with a Bluesman . . .
       A Bluesman.
       A Bluesman.

Doo doo doo
       Doo doo doo doo doo doo

CHICAGO (Has got everything you need)
Fernando Jones 6/8/98
©1992, 1998
Bluefunkjazroll Music, BMI

Chicago's got everything you need.
I said, 'Chicago's got everything you need.
We've got a Great Lake and gold plated streets.'

We've got hot dogs and championship teams.
I said, 'we've got Soul food and championship teams.
We're the city that works with a skyline that's mean.'

We've got theatres / and / movie shows.
For a couple of bucks / go where you wanna go.
I said, 'Chicago's got everything you need.
We've got a Great Lake and gold plated streets.'

Whenever I need a reason / a reason to smile.
I said, 'Whenever I need a reason / a reason to smile
I go window shoppin' on the Magnificent Mile.'

Chicago's got everything you need.
I said, 'Chicago's got everything you need.
We've got a Great Lake and gold plated streets.'

I Was There When The Blues Was Red Hot
Book in Review

Read these questions carefully and fill in the blanks. Revisit the chapters to help you with any of your answers. Have fun.

Tips: Take this lesson with your friends, family members, and/or classmates then compare and discuss your answers. You can even compile statistics for a pie chart.

1. Why do you think the Blues exists?
a. Because of the misusage of Africans enslaved in America.
b. It's a constant reminder of slavery and shouldn't be forgotten.
c. Rock & Roll, Jazz, Gospel, and Hip Hop exists, therefore, the Blues exists.

2. When you think of the Blues, what instrument comes to mind?
a. Guitar
b. Harmonica
c. Piano
d. Saxophone

Answer the next set of question using complete sentences.

3. How important is it to learn about different cultures through music?

_____

_____

_____

_____

4. How significant is the drum in African culture?

_____

_____

_____

_____

5. If you could write a song, what would you write about?

_____

_____

_____

_____

_____

Fernando Jones

6. Using the AAB format please share your song.

   A (Call)_____

   A (Response)_____

   B (Hook Line)_____

7. Name ten people in this book who may have changed the way you think about the Blues culturally and musically.

   _____

   _____

   _____

   _____

   _____

Vocabulary: What does the word mean in context of the sentence?

8. It's **ironic** that something so inhumane could produce an art form so beautiful.
   a. Nice
   b. Simple
   c. Contradictory

9. One of the **fundamentals** of Blues music is the call-and-response.
   a. Basics
   b. Differences
   c. Oddities

10. The drums **speak** to our spirit in a way nothing else can.
   a. Listens
   b. Talks
   c. Cry

8. = C; 9 = A; 10 = B

Write a 5 paragraph persuasive essay answering this prompt.

How important is the Blues from a sociological and historical perspective?

_____

_____

_____

_____

_____

_____

_____

_____

_____

_____

_____

_____

_____

_____

_____

_____

_____

_____

_____

_____

_____

Notes

Printed in the United States
23587LVS00002B/177-206